TO FROM

You Me

WITH

LOTS·OF·LOVE xx L

14.2.85

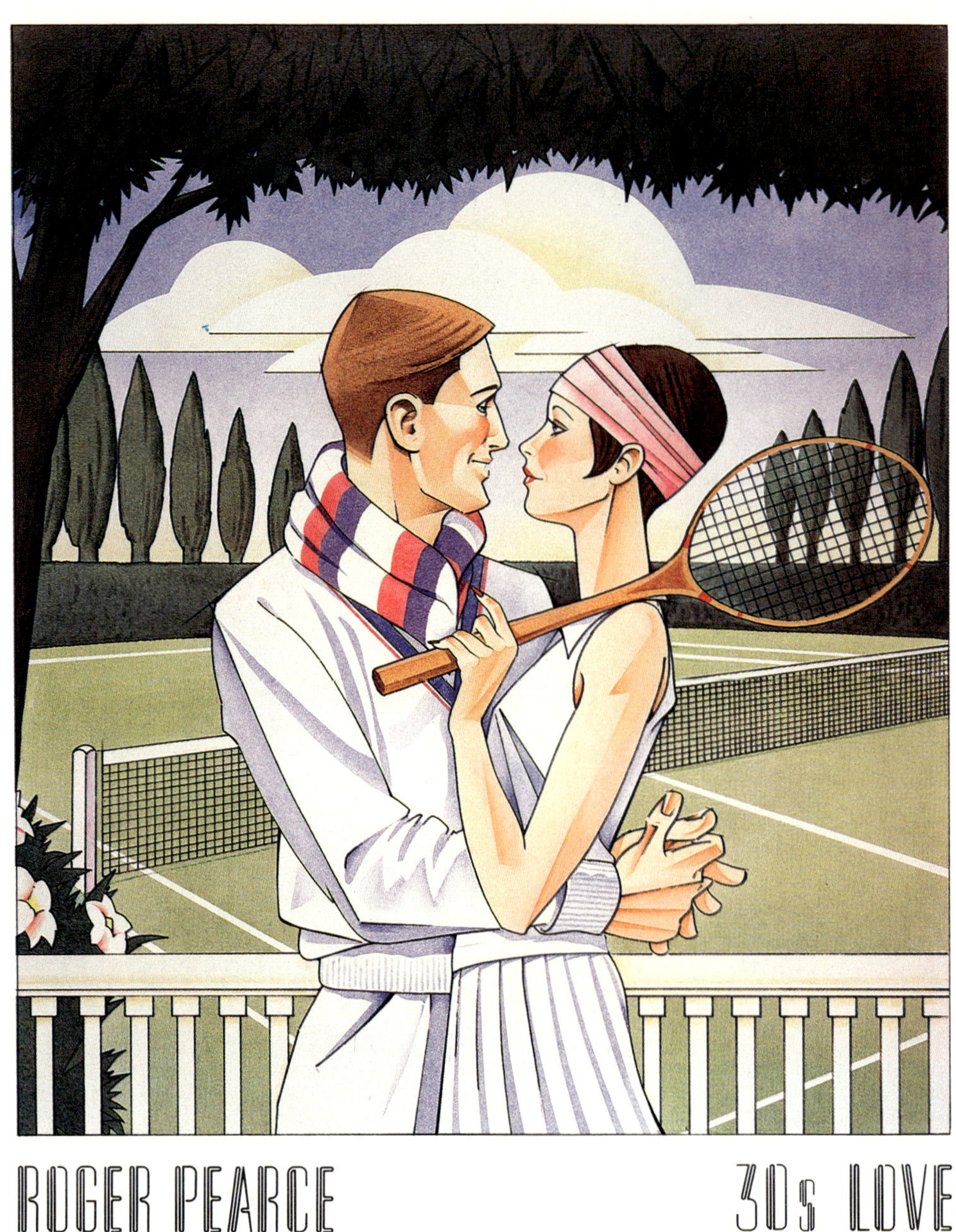
ROGER PEARCE
30s LOVE

LOTS·OF·LOVE

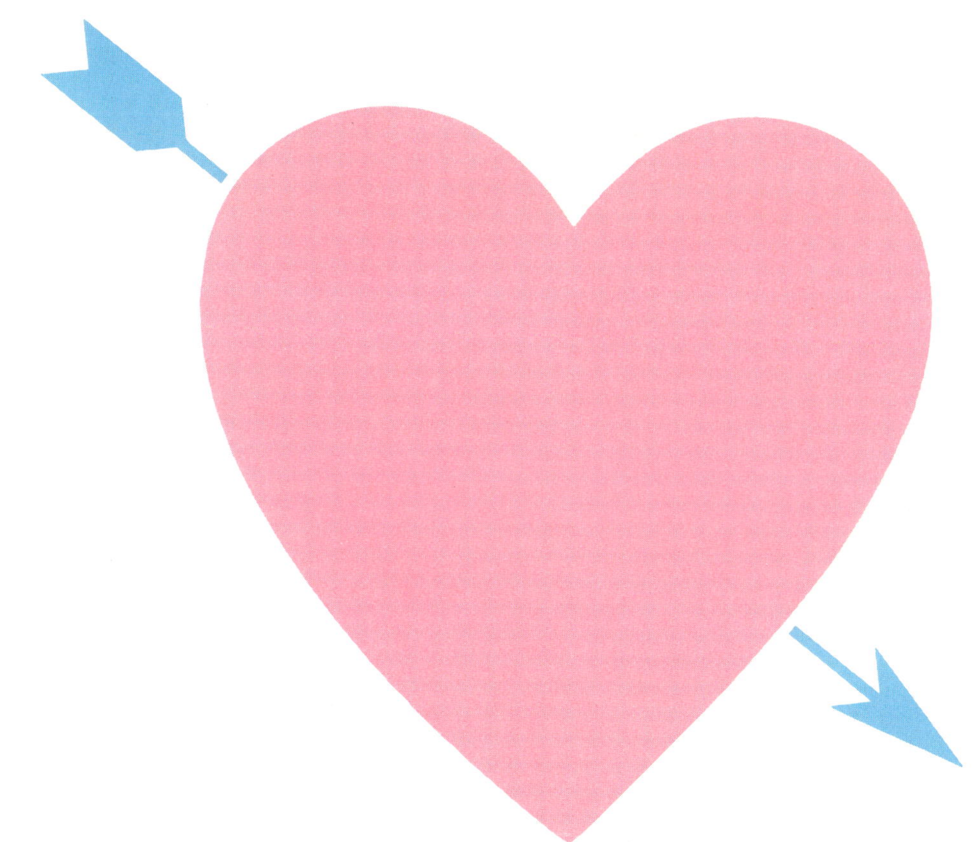

ILLUSTRATED BY MEIKLEJOHN ARTISTS

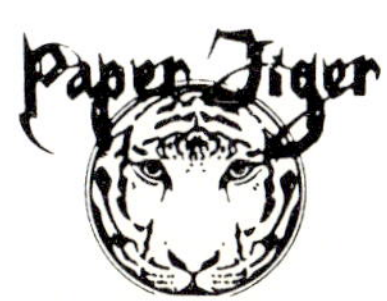

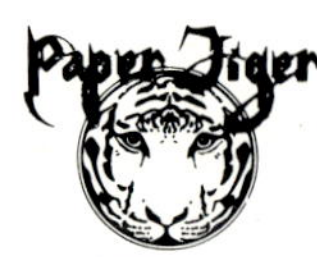

A Dragon's World Ltd Imprint

Dragon's World Ltd
Limpsfield
SURREY RH8 0DY
Great Britain

Designed by Simon Loxley

ISBN 0 905895 38 X

Printed in Italy

The Publishers wish to thank Chris Meiklejohn, of Meiklejohn Illustration, without whom this book would not have been possible.

30s Love · Roger Pearce
Love Letters in the Sand · Brian Robson
Love Pool · David Holmes
Food of Love · Pete Kelly
Not for Love or Money · Phil Littler
Lovers' Leap · Keith Laban
Love on the Rocks · Pete Kelly
Love Bite · Irvine Peacock
Nature Lover · Gavin Macleod
Love is Blind · John Mac
Good Night Love · Brian Robson
Tons of Love · Roger Pearce
Animal Love · Andrew Farley
Midnight Love · Gareth Williams
Love Foreseen · Andrew Farley
Young Love · David Holmes
For Love of the Dance · Syd Brak
I Love New York · Brian James
Love Me · Brian Robson
Hopeless Love · John Mac
Love's Rendezvous · Paul Simmons
Fine Art Lovers · Warren Madill
Two Love · Gavin Macleod
Dream Lover · Steve Gulbis
Cruise Love · Roger Pearce
The Love of Luxury · John Mac
The Art of Love · Paul Simmons
Love Story · Ian Bott/Pete Kelly
Forget-Me-Not · Syd Brak
Love Shaker, Heartbreaker · Roger Pearce
Oriental Love · Ian Bott/Pete Kelly
Lovedroid · Barry Lepard
Love Express · Brian James
Everyone Loves a Hero · Barry Lepard
Lost Love · John Mac
Love Remembered · Syd Brak
Love Potion · Gerry Preston

"We love being in love," wrote W. M. Thackeray in *Henry Esmond,* and how right he was. What a delicious feeling it is, that tender arrow through the heart. There's nothing like it, nothing else which makes life so worth living, and no wonder so much time and energy is spent trying to draw the invisible archer's fire. To be indifferent to love is to be indifferent to life itself.

But what do we mean by love?

We mean whatever we want to mean . . . usually romance. Boy meets girl in the movies – or *at* the movies – and they walk off together into the sunset's rosy glow, hand-in-hand on a windswept beach, or running blissfully through a summer meadow, never stepping in any of the unpleasant surprises summer meadows are so full of.

That may be the popular, public image, but everyone has a personal picture. "Common as light is love," the poet Shelley proclaimed, and he might well have added, just as necessary. It could hardly be restricted to the young and beautiful: love is at once the most private experience, and the most universal.

The Eskimo have seven distinctly different words to describe snow. Although, to someone from a more temperate latitude, all that cold white stuff looks the same, to an Eskimo snow is too important, too much a part of life, to be summed up by one word, as if it were all the same. Logically, we should have at least as many words for love as the Eskimos have for snow – or as we have for trees. Yet we make do with only one. No wonder people misunderstand each other!

(The Eskimos, by the way, may be no better than we are when it comes to naming love, but they do have some happy metaphors: what we call "making love" is to them "laughing together.")

We use the same word to stand for passion, affection and everything in between; by *love* we may mean something as comforting as a child's worn teddy bear, as painful as the memory of lost happiness, as lavish as a wealthy and mythical past, as ordinary and as magical as two people finding each other and staying together against all odds.

The connections made by love may be baffling to an outsider, so that we say "Love is blind." But the truth is that love is not blindness, but vision, for it instills the power of seeing in a new and different way, perhaps more clearly, perhaps more deeply, but at the very least from another perspective. Where the world in general sees a shaggy, funny-looking creature, a lover perceives the soul beneath the shagginess . . . and also, perhaps, the shagginess of her own soul.

But the feelings between two people is not all there is to love. The arrow that strikes the heart doesn't have to be fired by another person. Perhaps love is best shared, but it can be a solitary pursuit as well: a bittersweet memory, an unrequited desire, a dream, or the self-satisfaction of hard work, of goals achieved, of giving yourself over to an experience, heart and soul. Whatever the cause, wherever it comes from, love is a divine madness.

What except madness – or love – could explain the behavior of a sailor? The way common sense, comfort, safety and the family fortunes become unimportant, and a small boat becomes the center of a universe which is mostly water. You couldn't call sailing a hobby, for people don't alter their whole lives for something as trivial as a hobby, but they will for love. And can anything in the years ahead really compare with the intensity of passion felt by a nine-year-old girl for an imaginary horse?

Places, too, can exert a powerful emotional attraction, as all those bumper stickers with hearts on them attest. Whether your inclinations lead you to the glitter and noise of a big city, or to an old house slumbering in a remote valley, there are certain landscapes which pierce the heart, places you visit once and dream of forever after, or spend your life trying to find again – and that, too, is love.

Examples could be piled up for pages more without providing a definition of love. The mystery is part of love's allure. Everyone knows what love is when they feel it, but few can define it. It seems to mean something different to everyone, yet there must be something which makes all these different experiences a part of the same thing.

No doubt there are scientists somewhere, inspired by love of knowledge, determined to break love down to its chemical constituents, whether to provide a cure (after all, it can be so inconvenient if the wrong person falls in love at the wrong time!) or to be able to create it at will.

It's easy enough to imagine a science fiction scenario with love-essence sold in bottles to the rich, or doled out by a repressive government to the deserving few, but it's impossible to believe such a state of affairs could last. Love, after all, doesn't play by the rules. Love is wild and unexpected, irrational and free. Perhaps love can be imitated or induced, but it can't be confined. There will always be rebellious lovers, people – and perhaps even robots and computers in the future – who fall in love without permission, against all laws and logic.

The heart has its own rules, and they can only be described, not defined. Millions upon millions of words have been written about love without changing it. For poets, novelists, playwrights, composers, filmmakers, songwriters, and artists of all kinds, love is the great and inexhaustible subject. The creation of a work of art can itself be an act of love: remember the story of Pygmalion, who in creating the image of love, fell in love with it?

Images do have that power, and that great advantage over words. Like music, beautiful pictures shoot straight to the heart. The pictures in this book all suggest different aspects of love and, better than merely defining it, they may remind you how it feels.

Lisa Tuttle

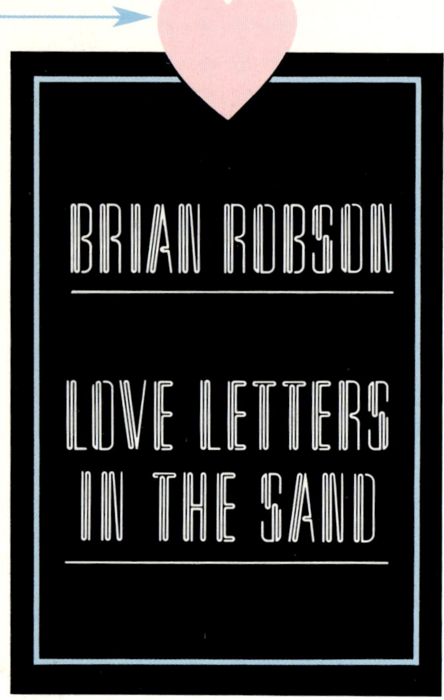
BRIAN ROBSON
LOVE LETTERS
IN THE SAND

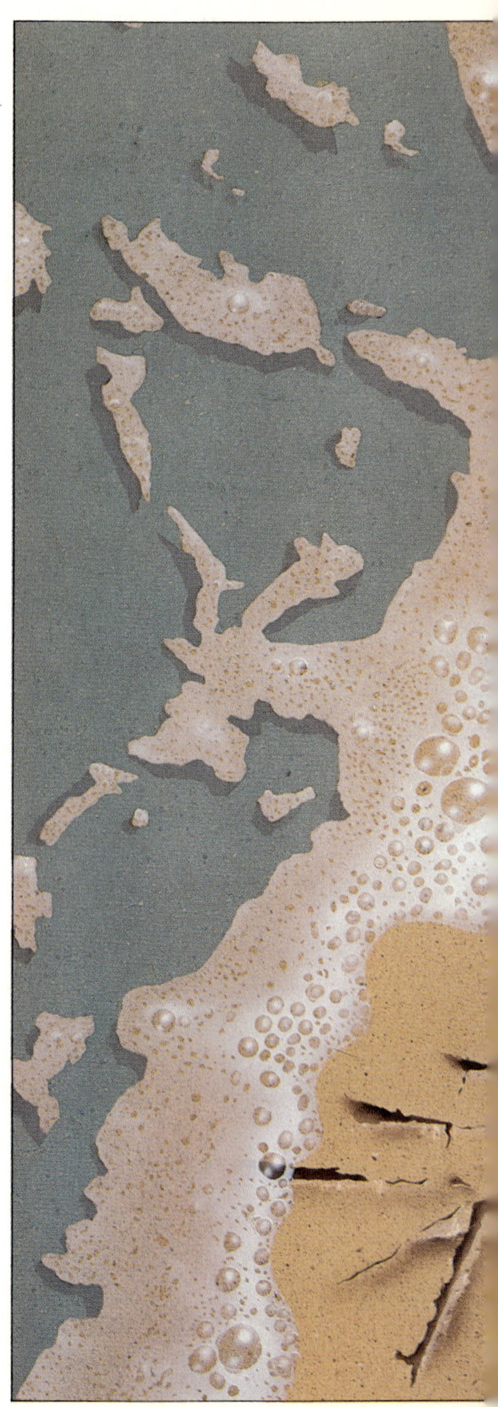

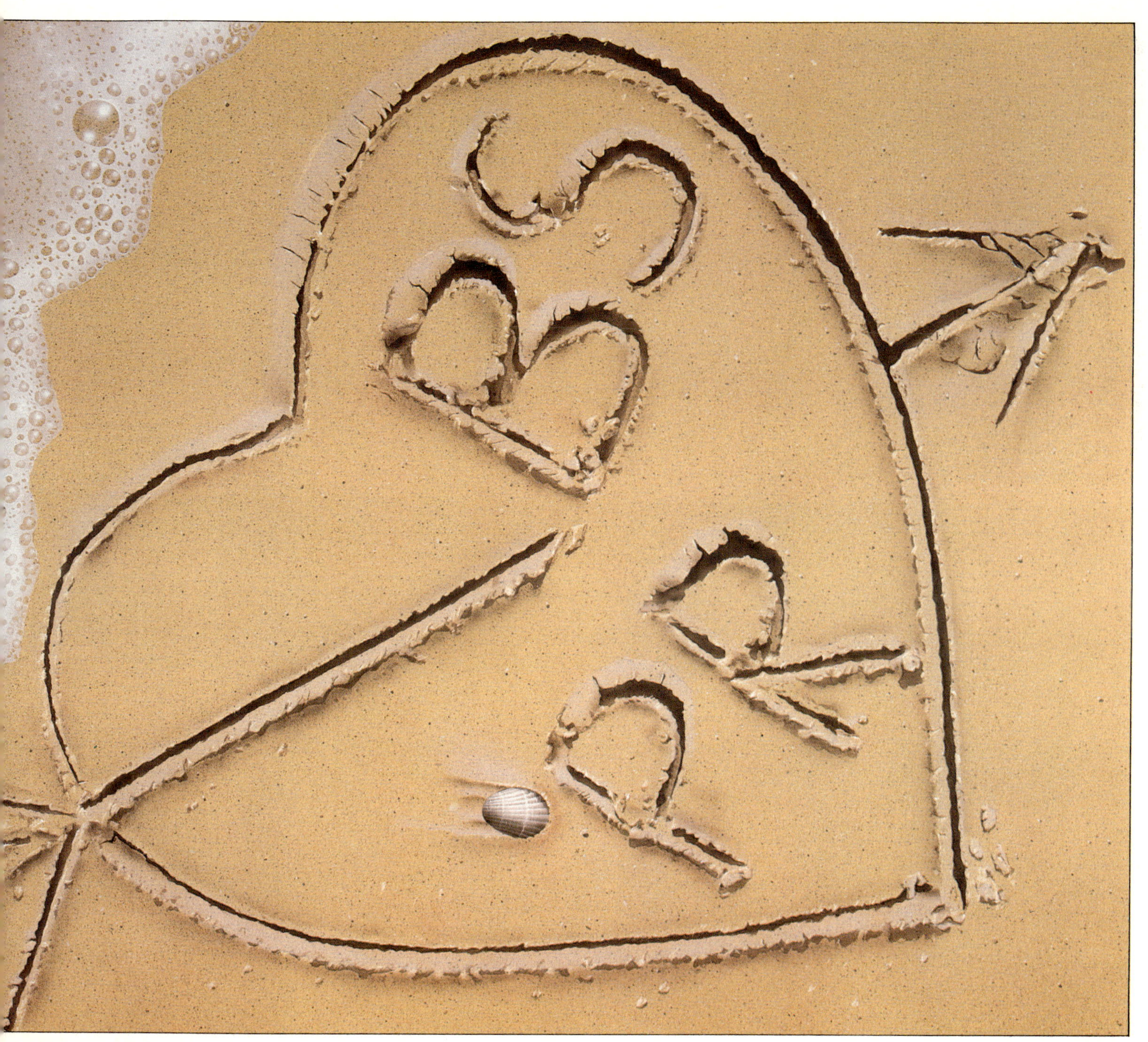

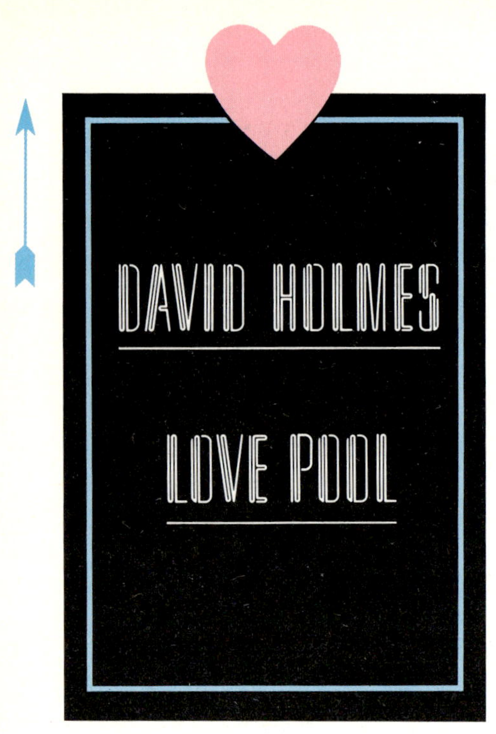
DAVID HOLMES
LOVE POOL

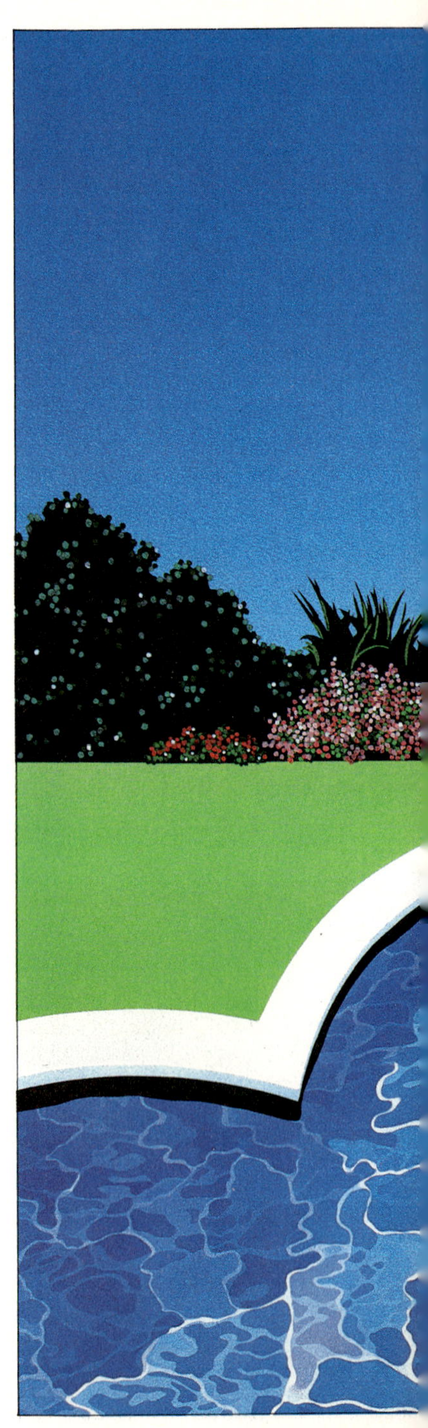

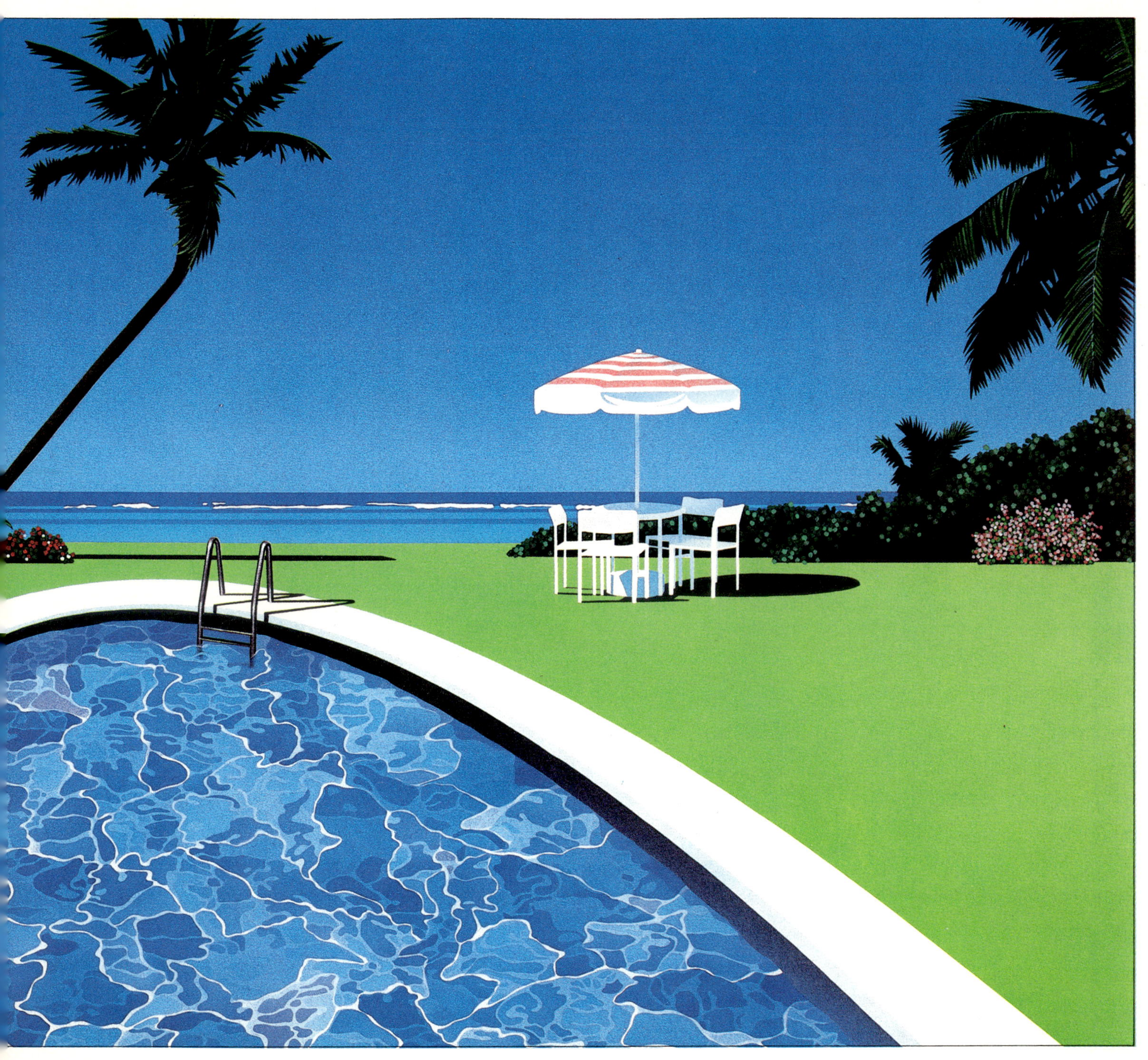

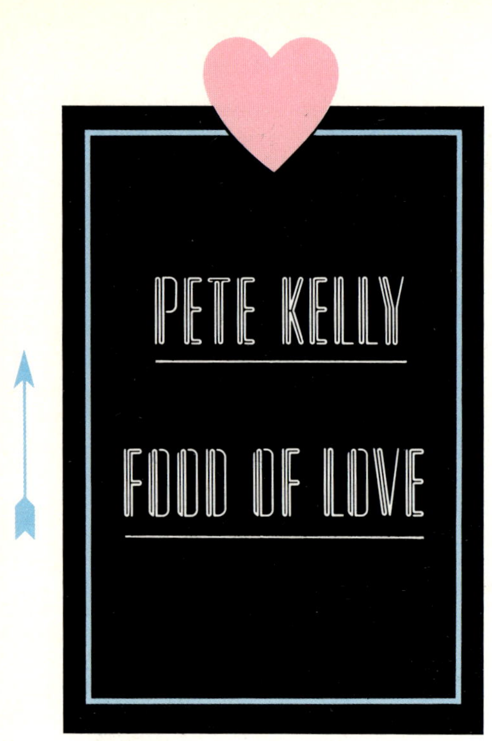
PETE KELLY
FOOD OF LOVE

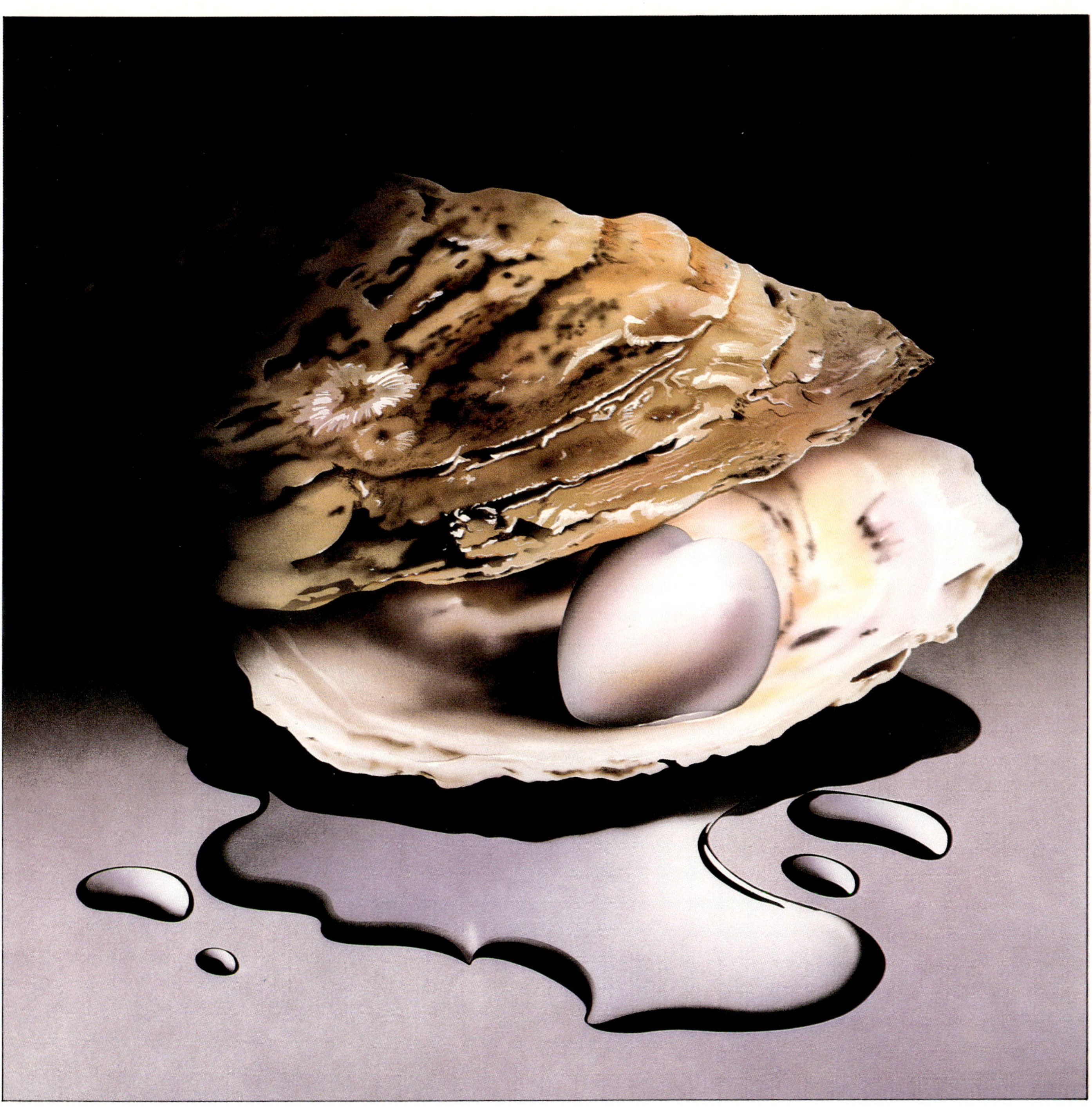

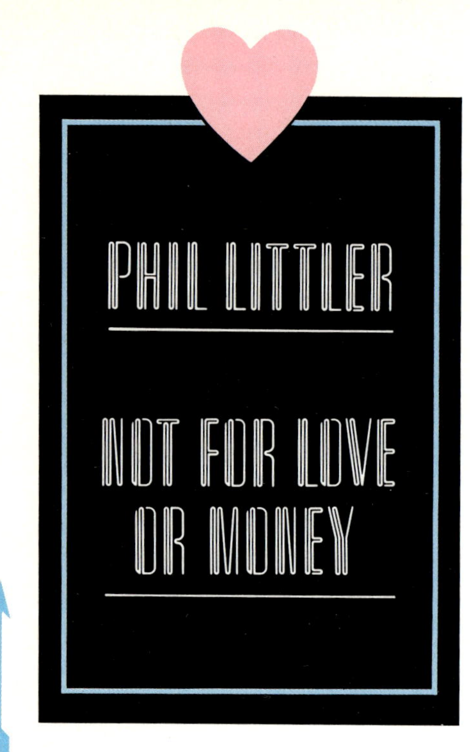
PHIL LITTLER
NOT FOR LOVE
OR MONEY

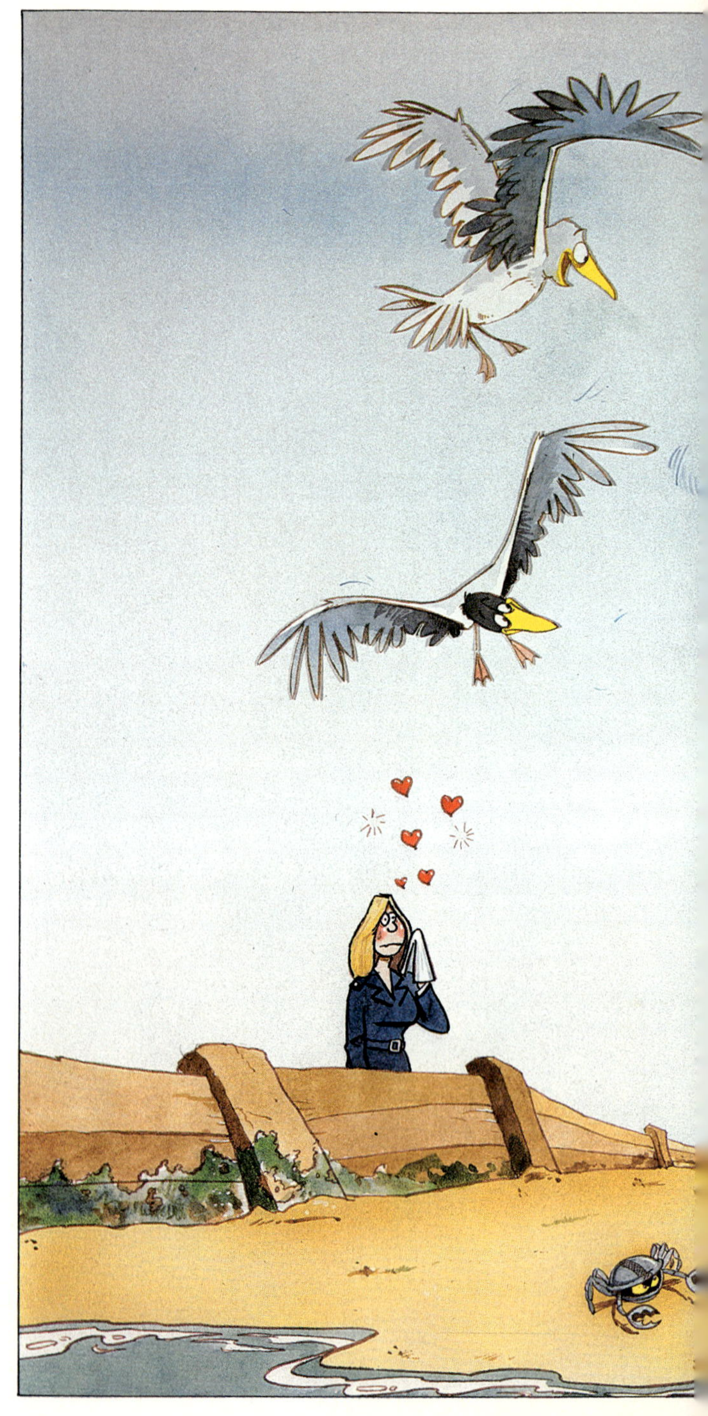

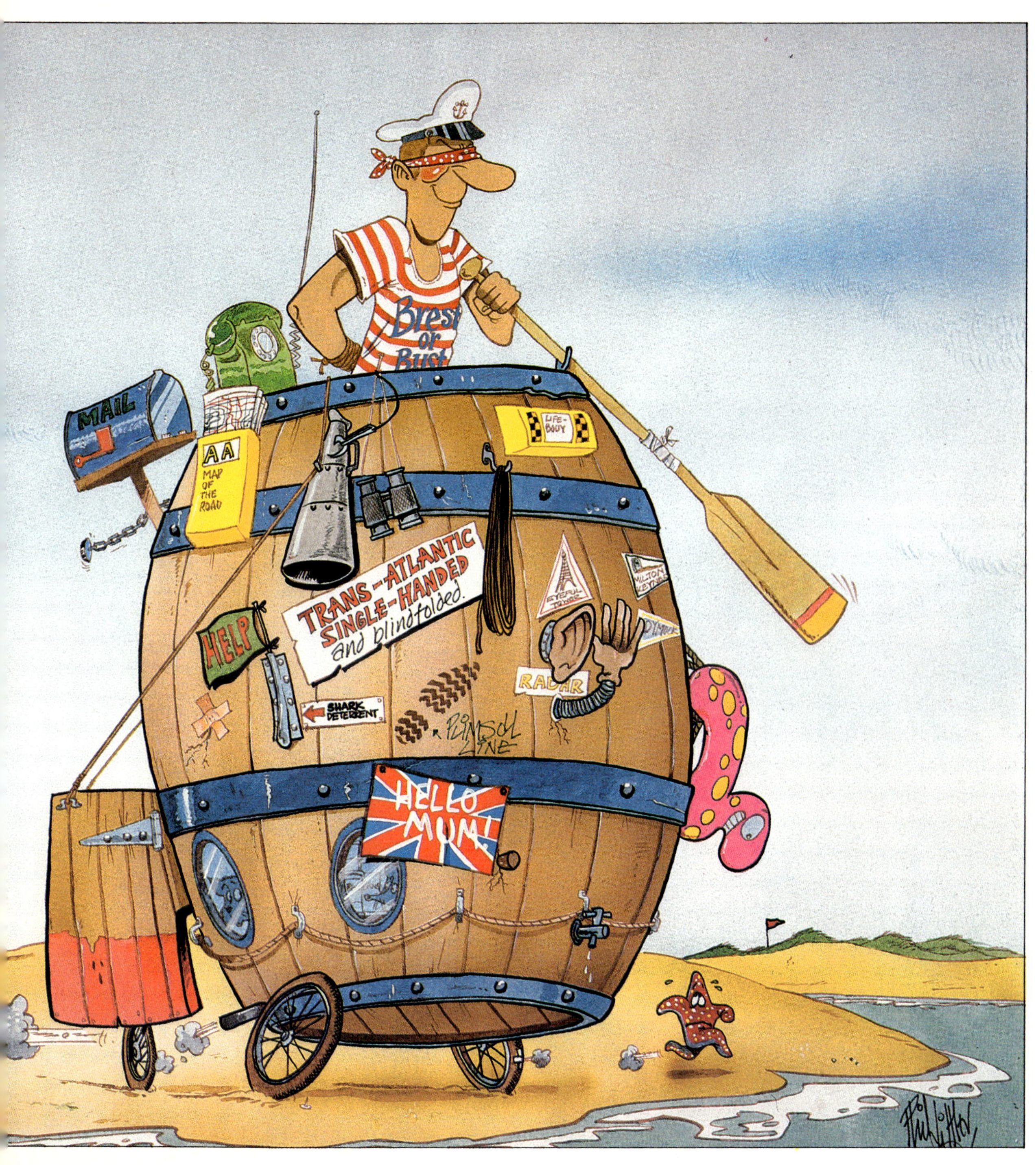

Brest or Bust
MAIL
AA
MAP OF THE ROAD
LIFE-BUOY
TRANS-ATLANTIC SINGLE-HANDED
and blindfolded.
HELP
EYEFUL TOWER
MILTON KEYNES
RADAR
SHARK DETERRENT
PLIMSOLL LINE
HELLO MUM!

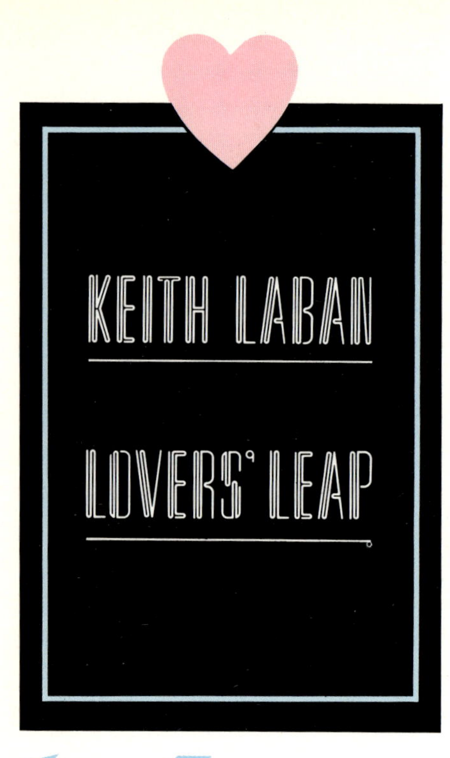
KEITH LABAN
LOVERS' LEAP

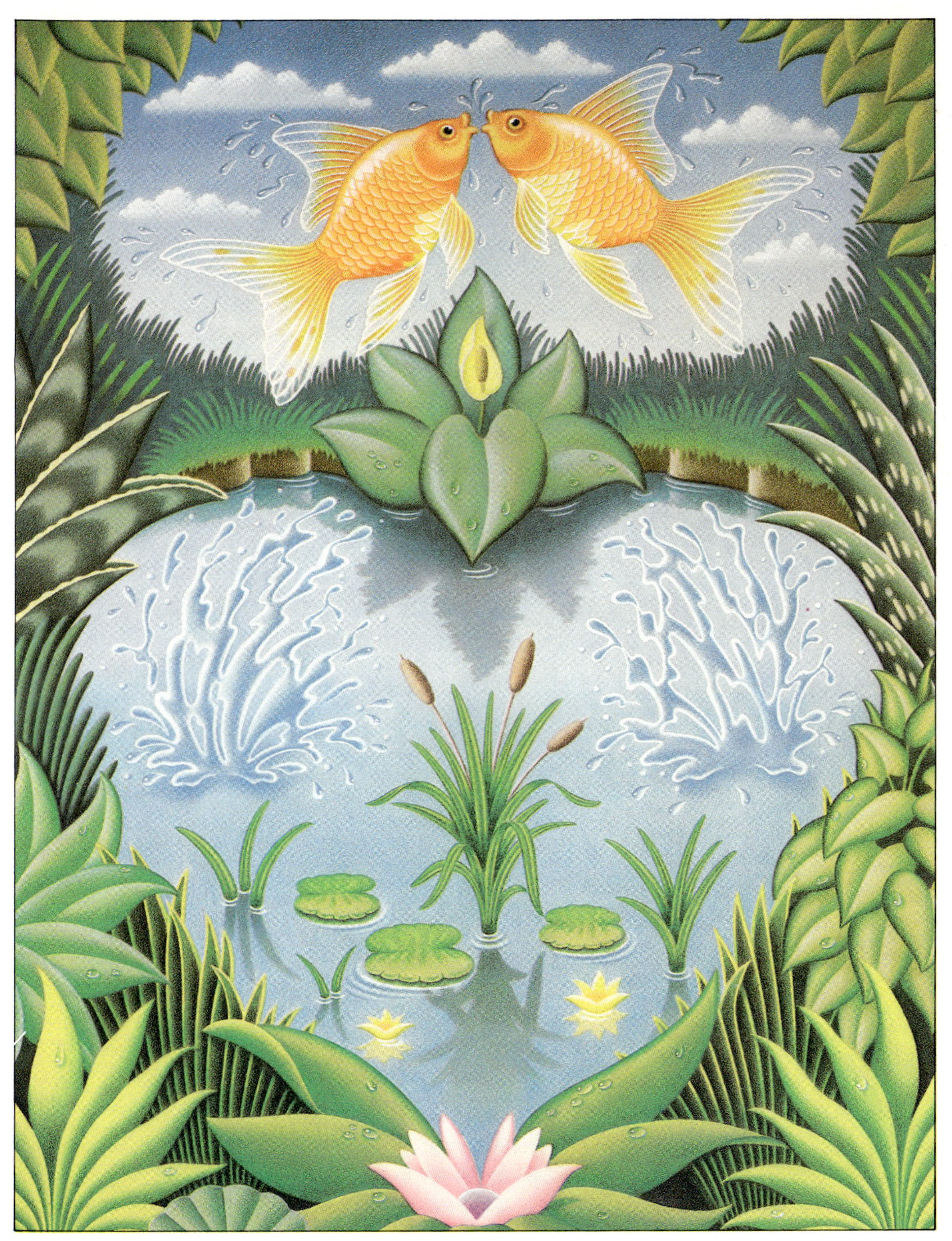

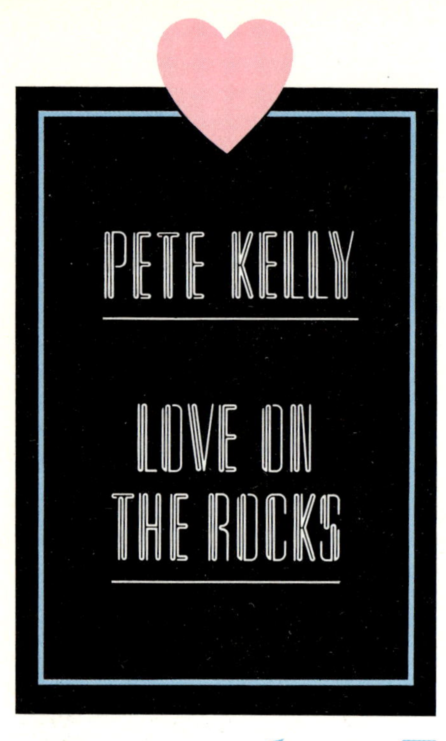
PETE KELLY
LOVE ON THE ROCKS

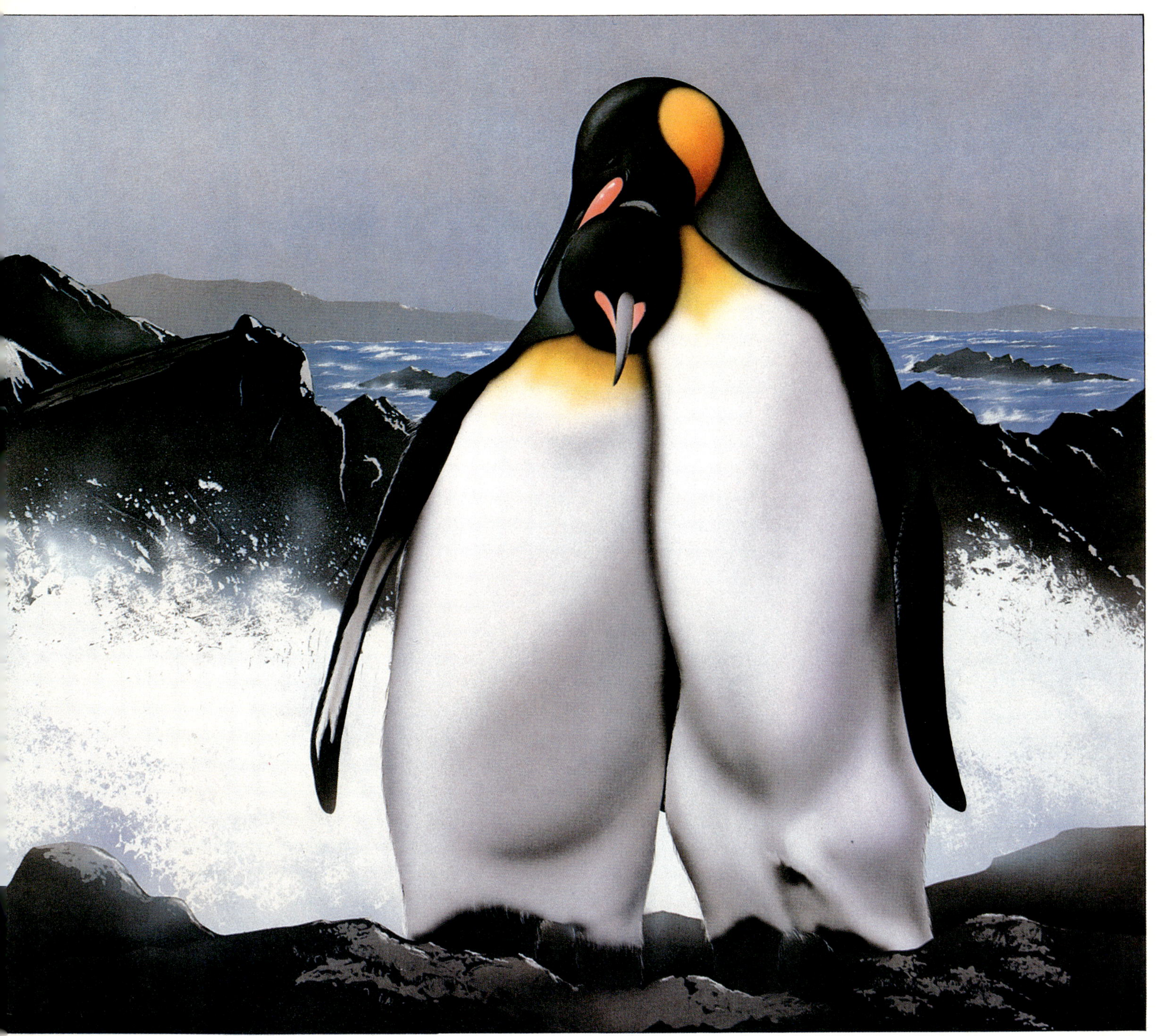

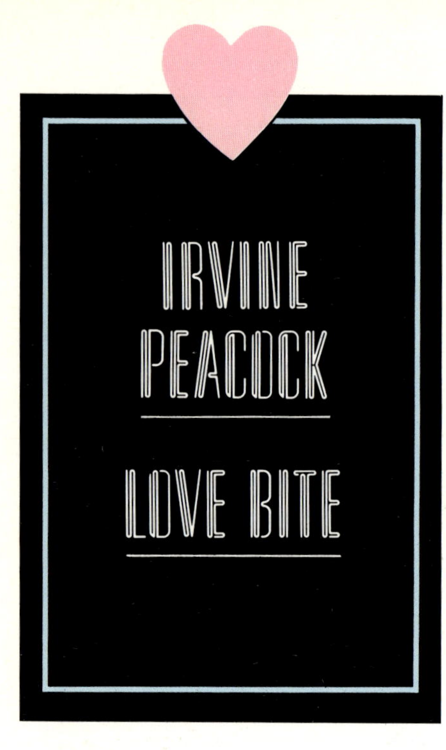
IRVINE
PEACOCK
LOVE BITE

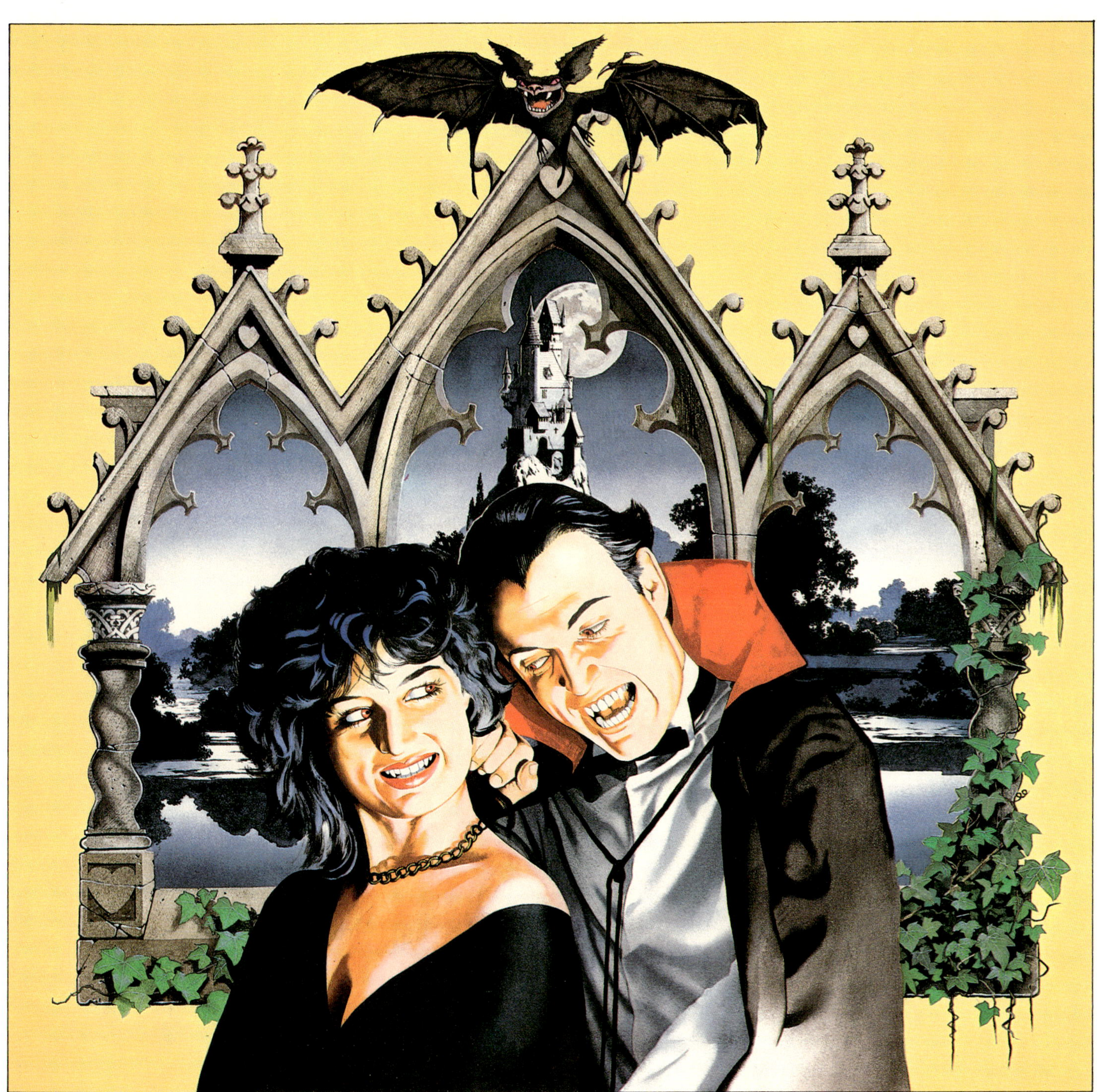

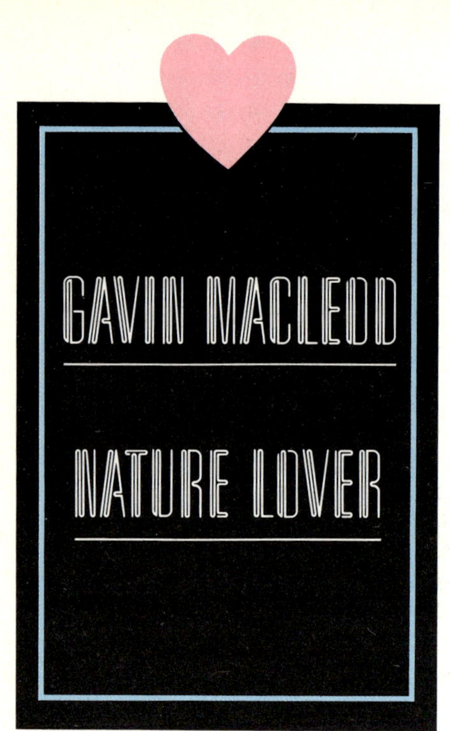
GAVIN MACLEOD
NATURE LOVER

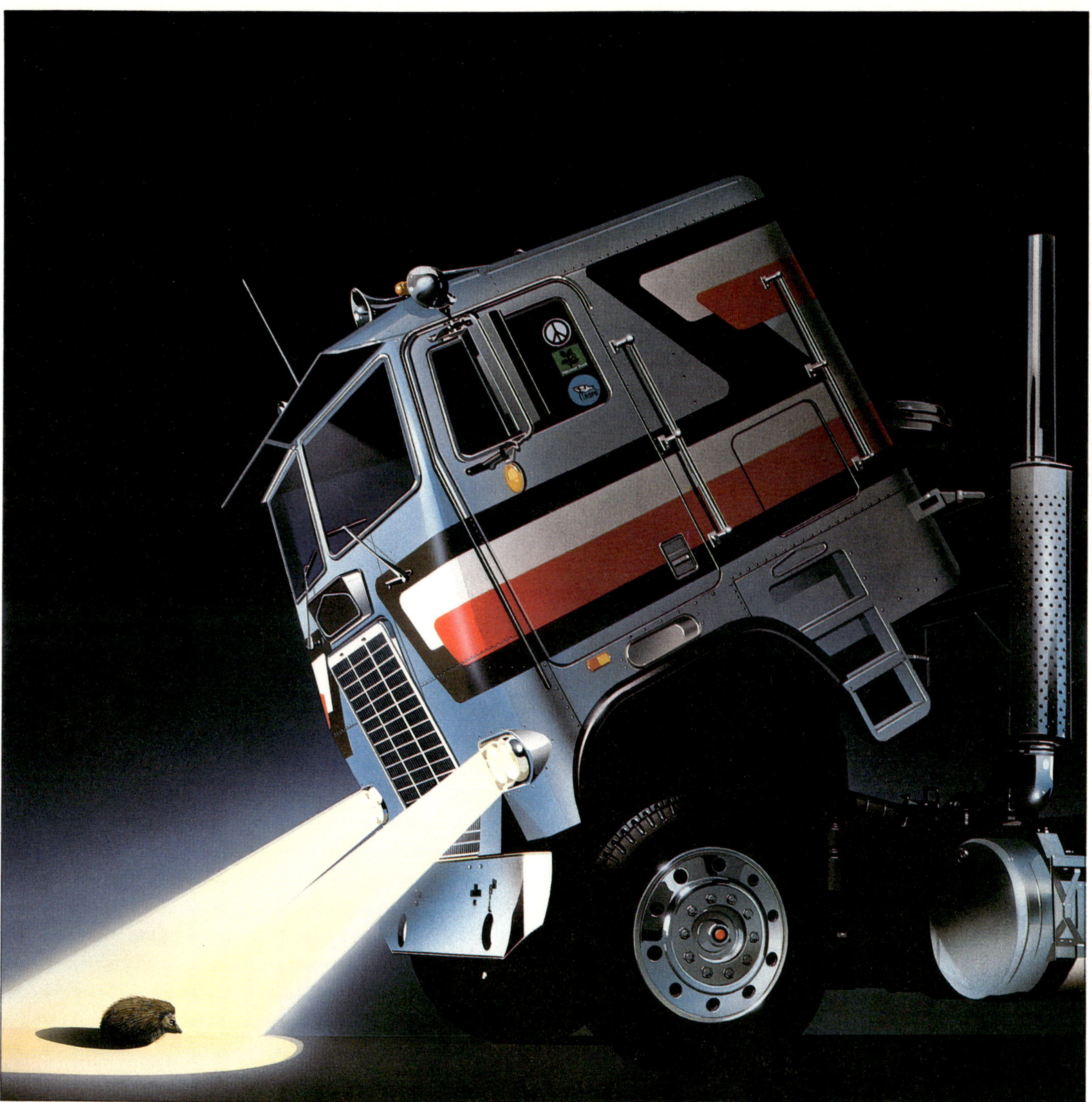

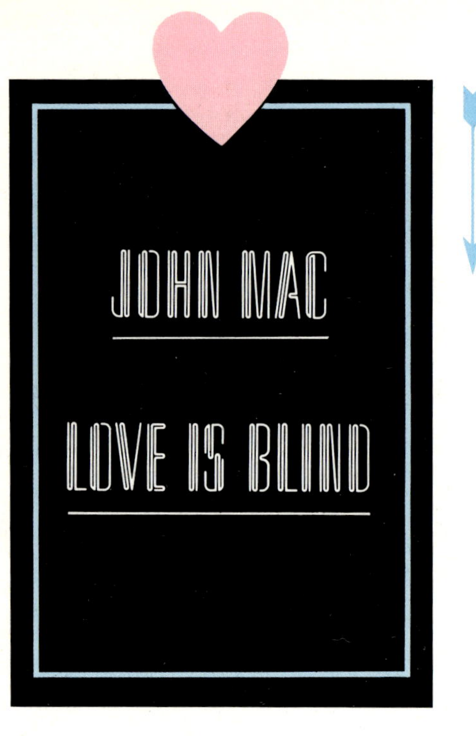
JOHN MAC
LOVE IS BLIND

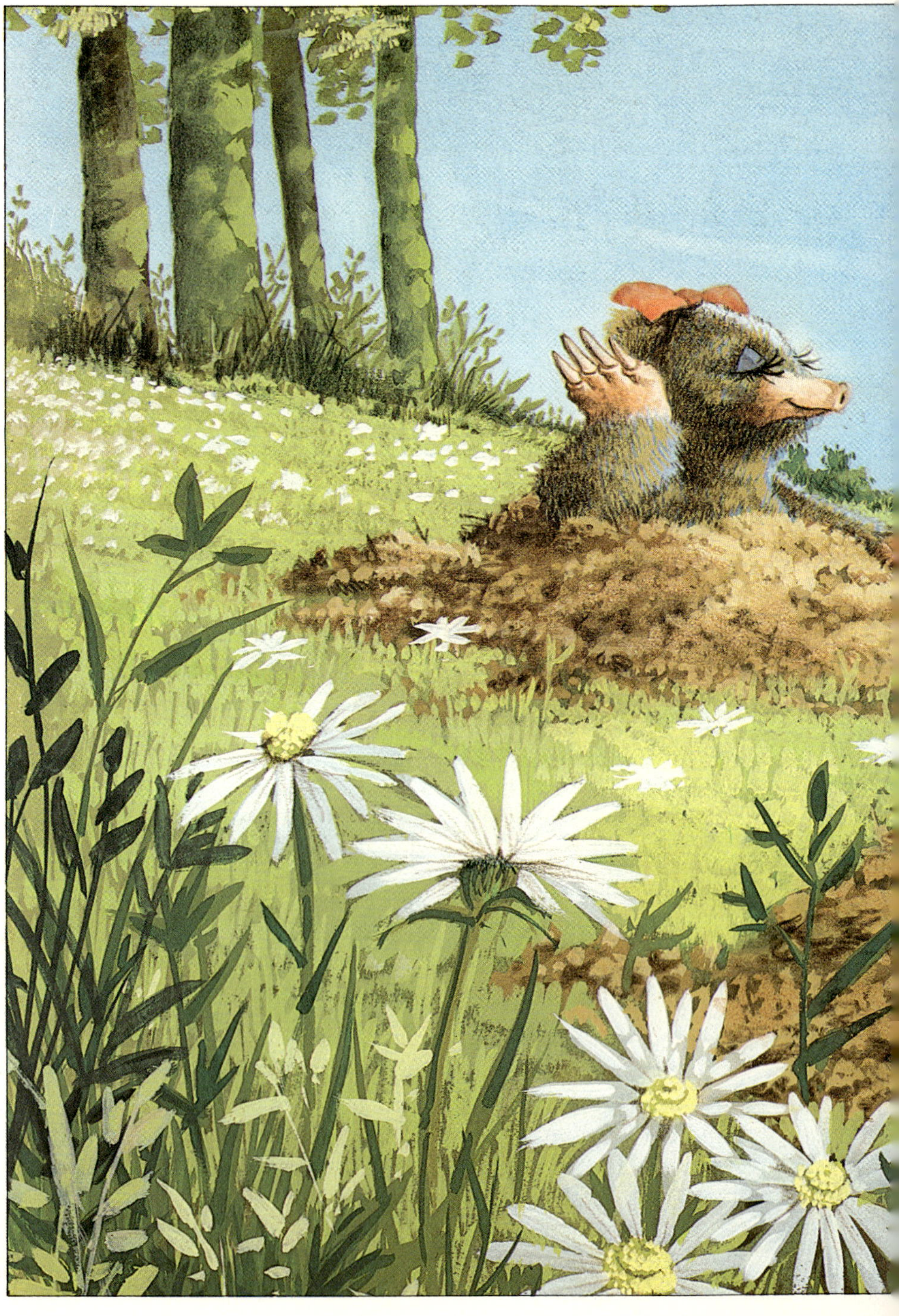

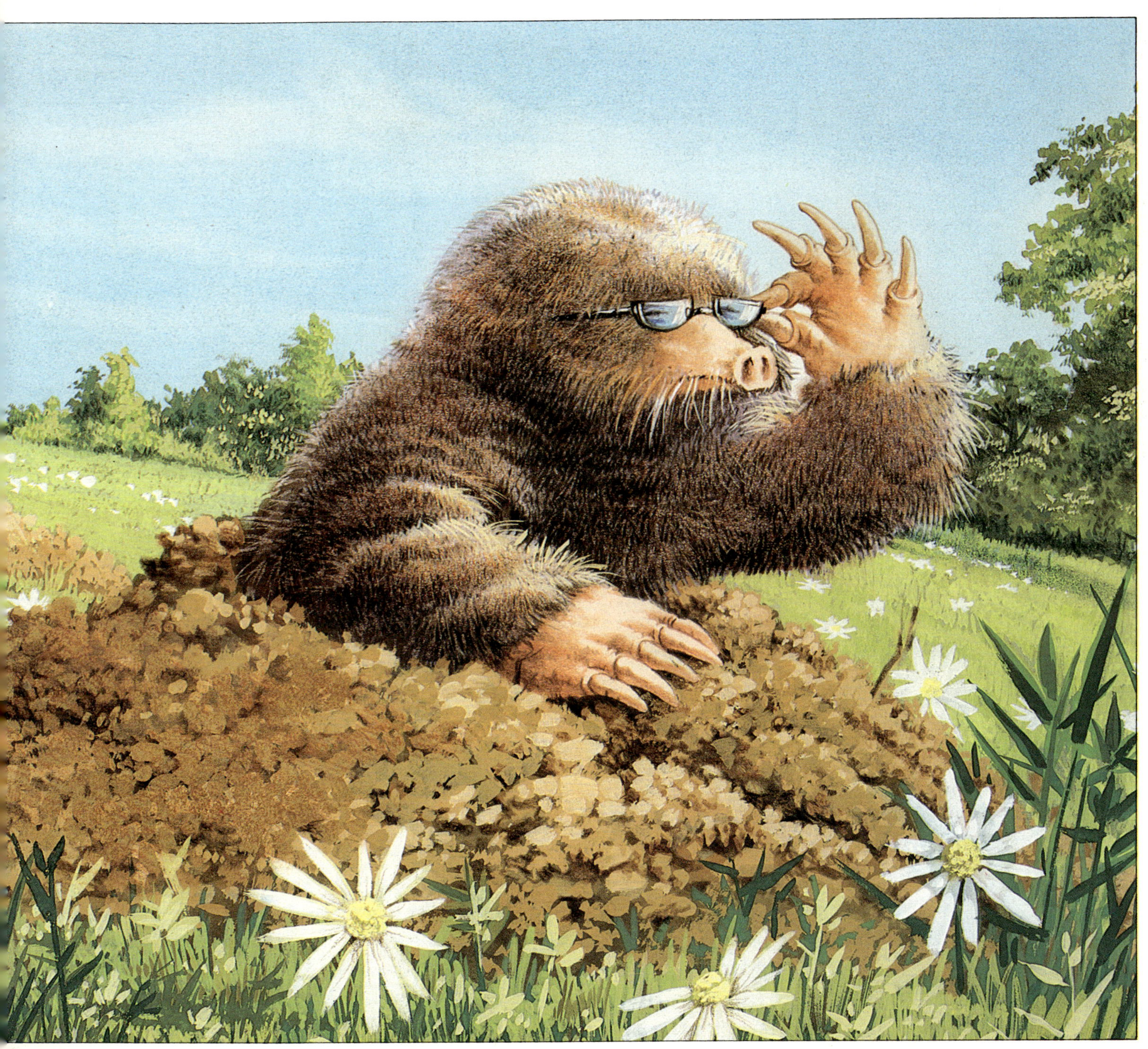

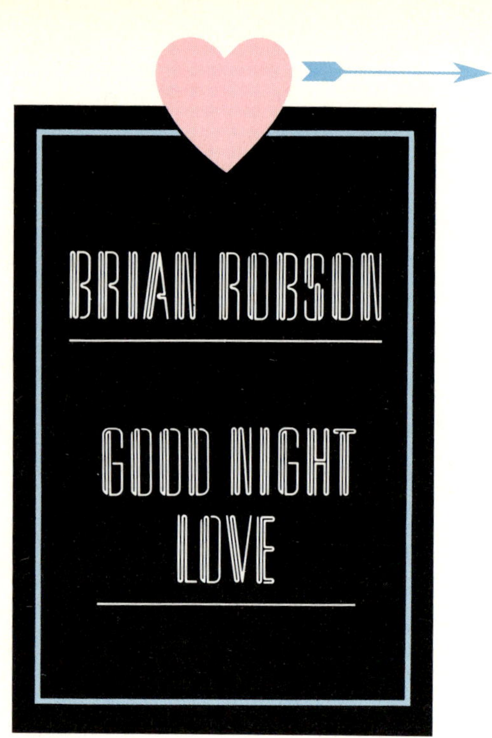
BRIAN ROBSON
GOOD NIGHT
LOVE

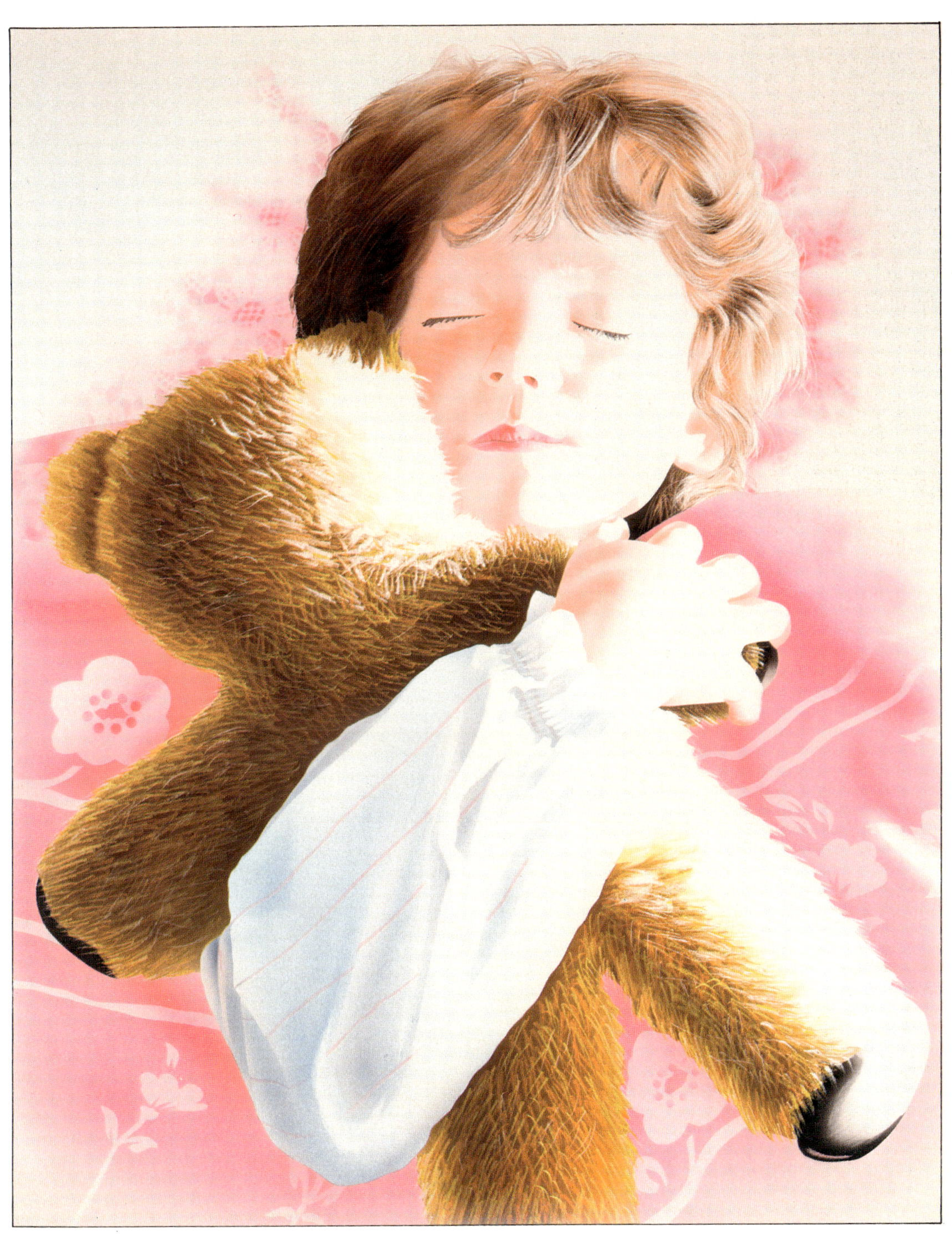

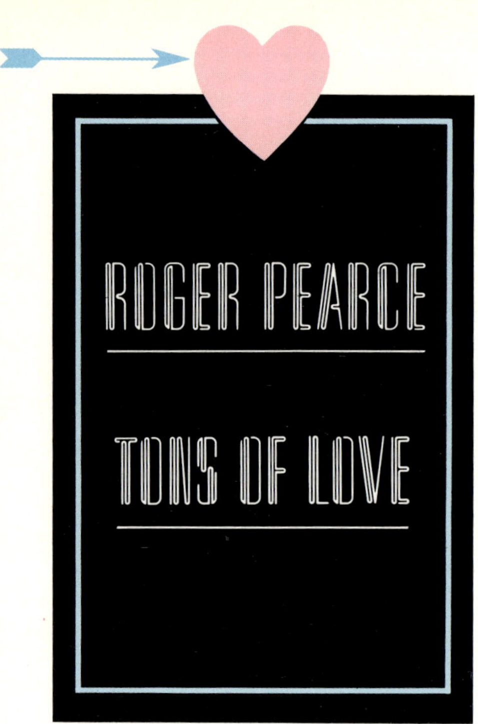
ROGER PEARCE
TONS OF LOVE

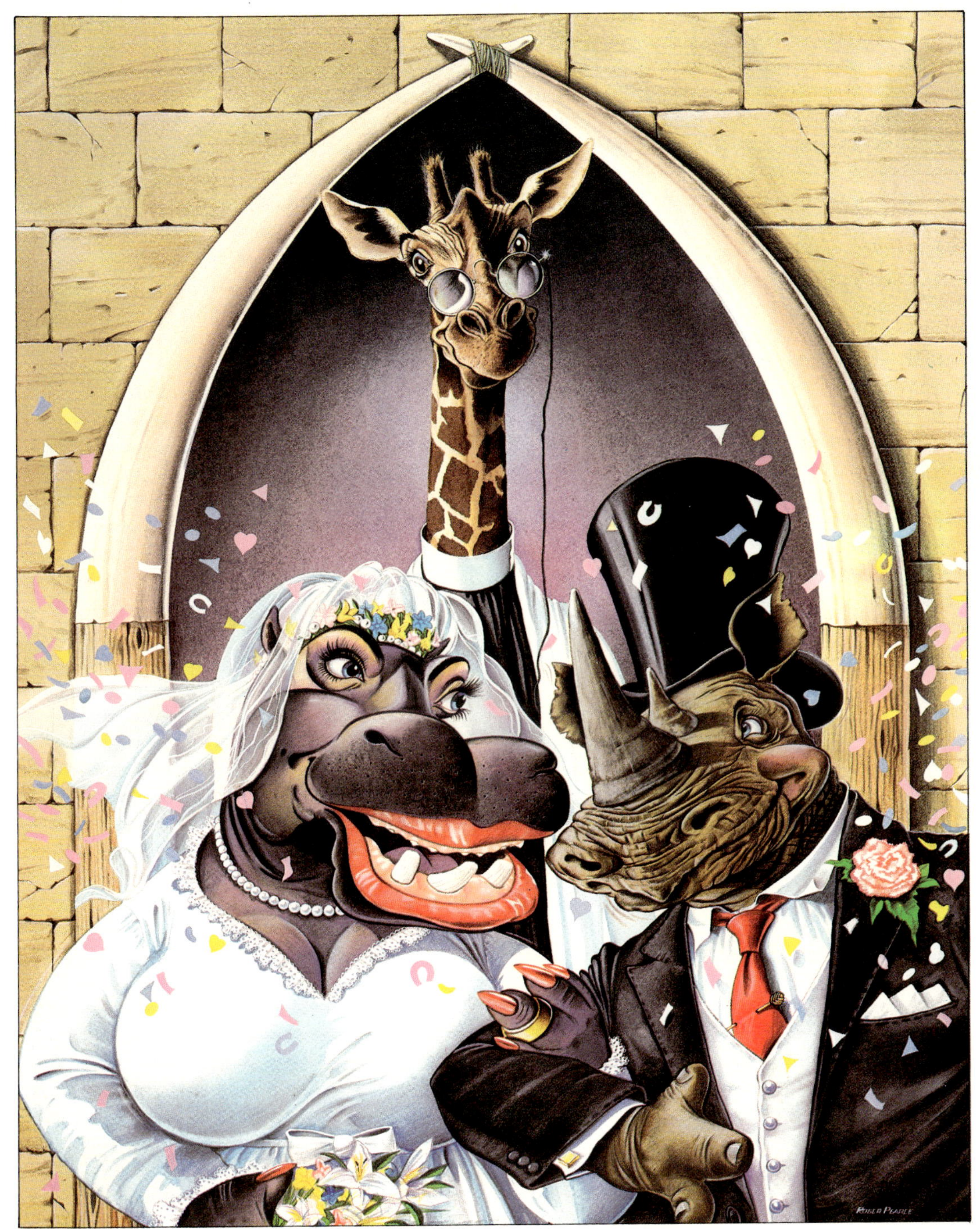

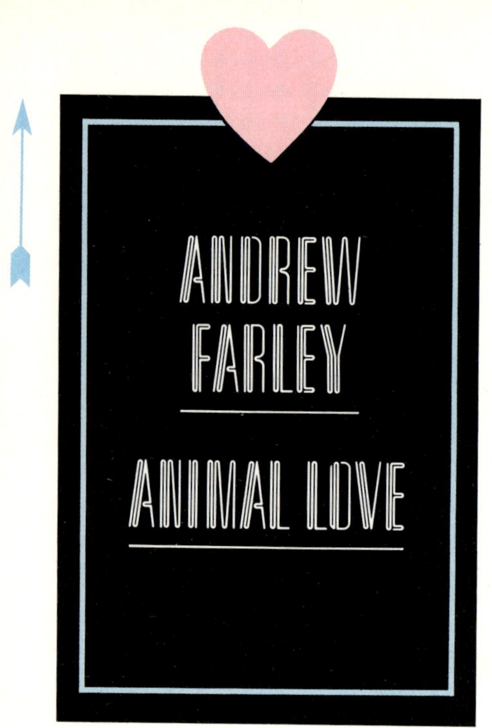
ANDREW
FARLEY
ANIMAL LOVE

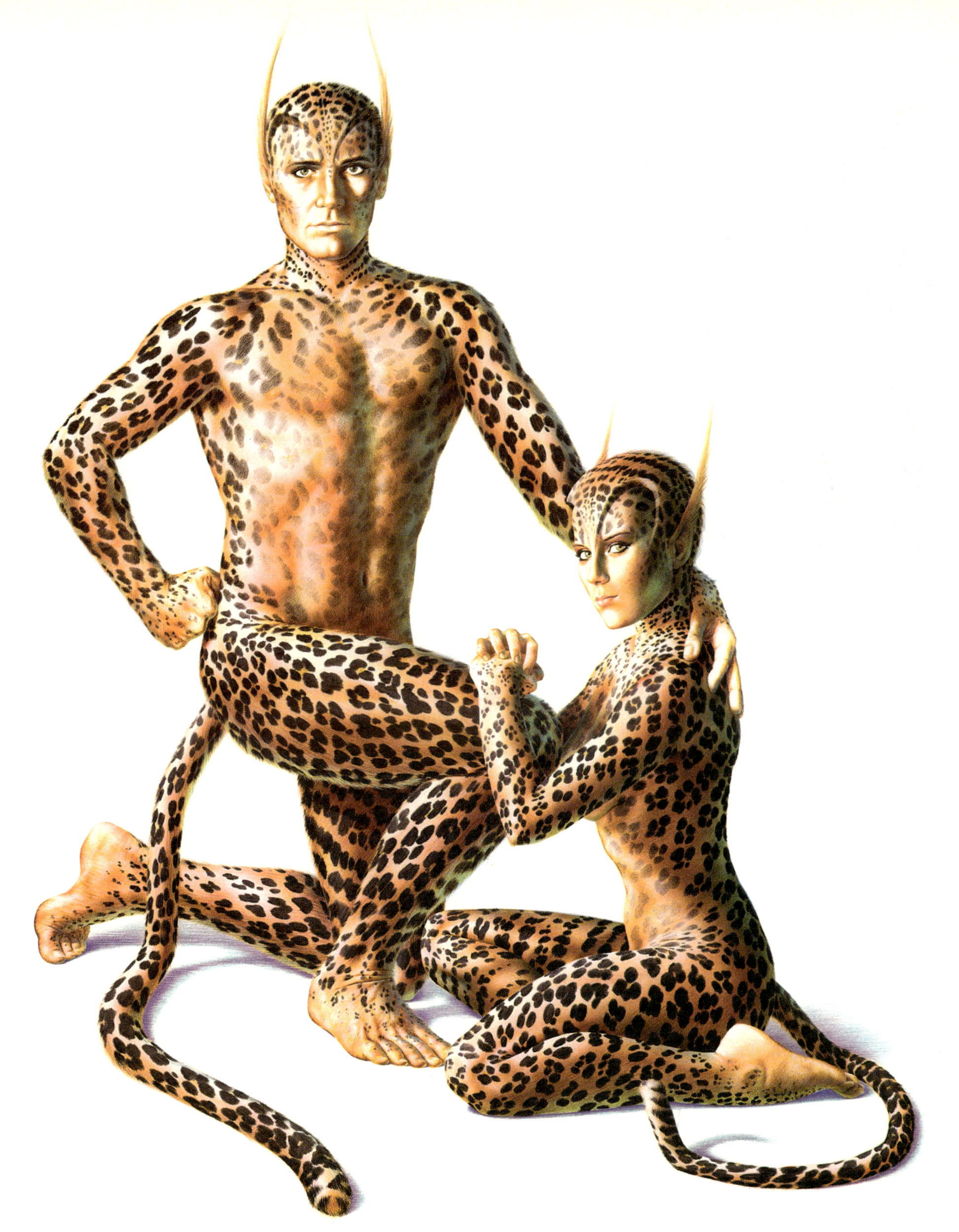

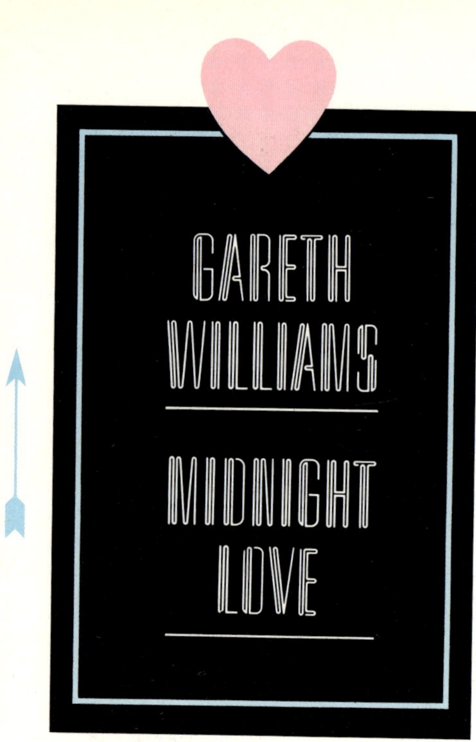
GARETH
WILLIAMS
MIDNIGHT
LOVE

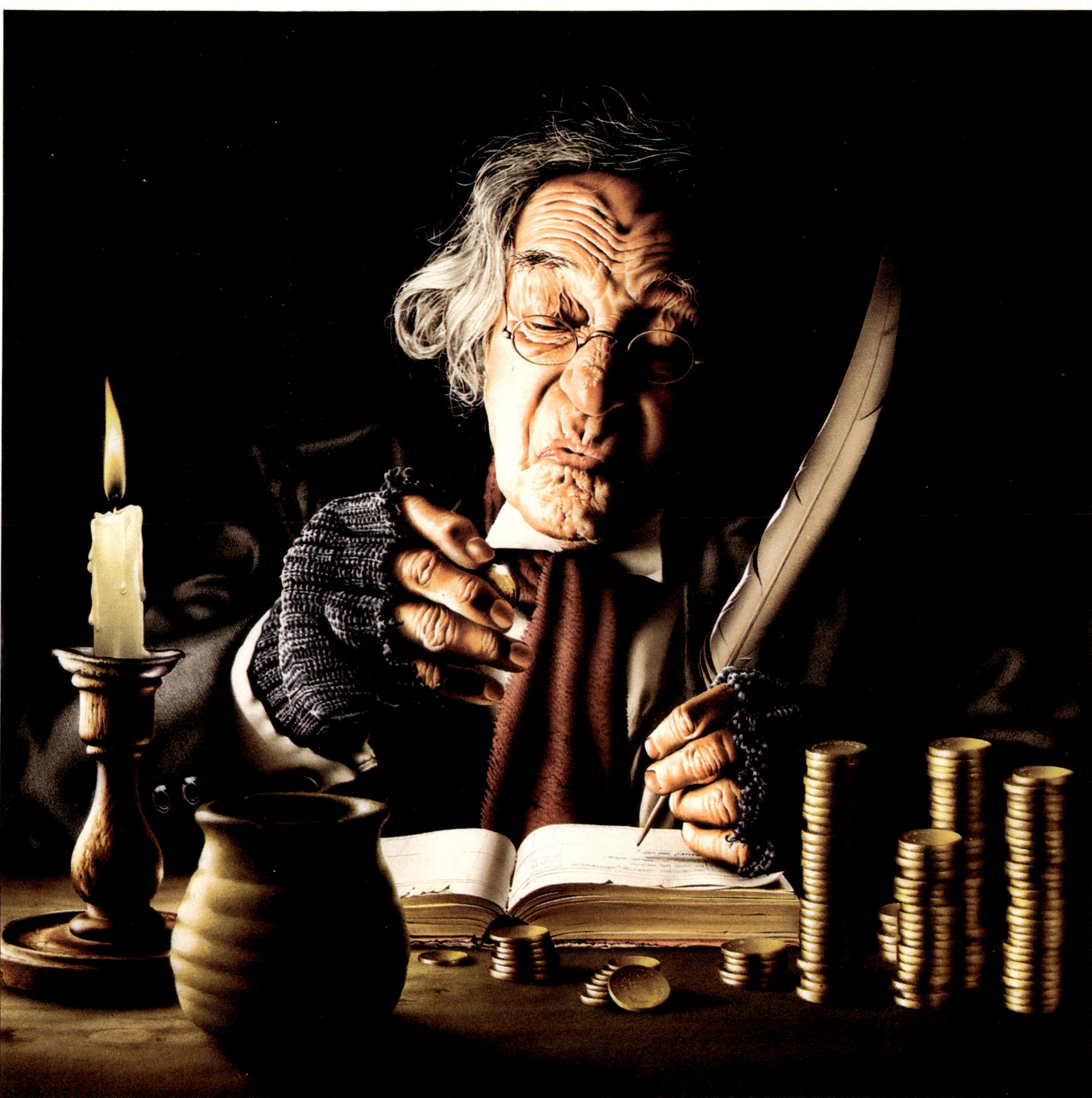

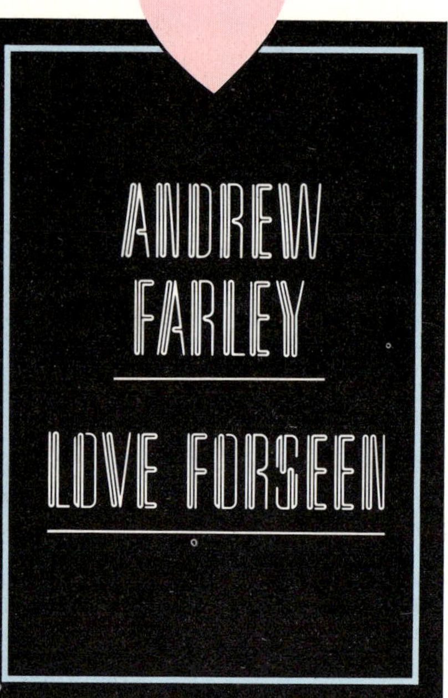
ANDREW
FARLEY
LOVE FORSEEN

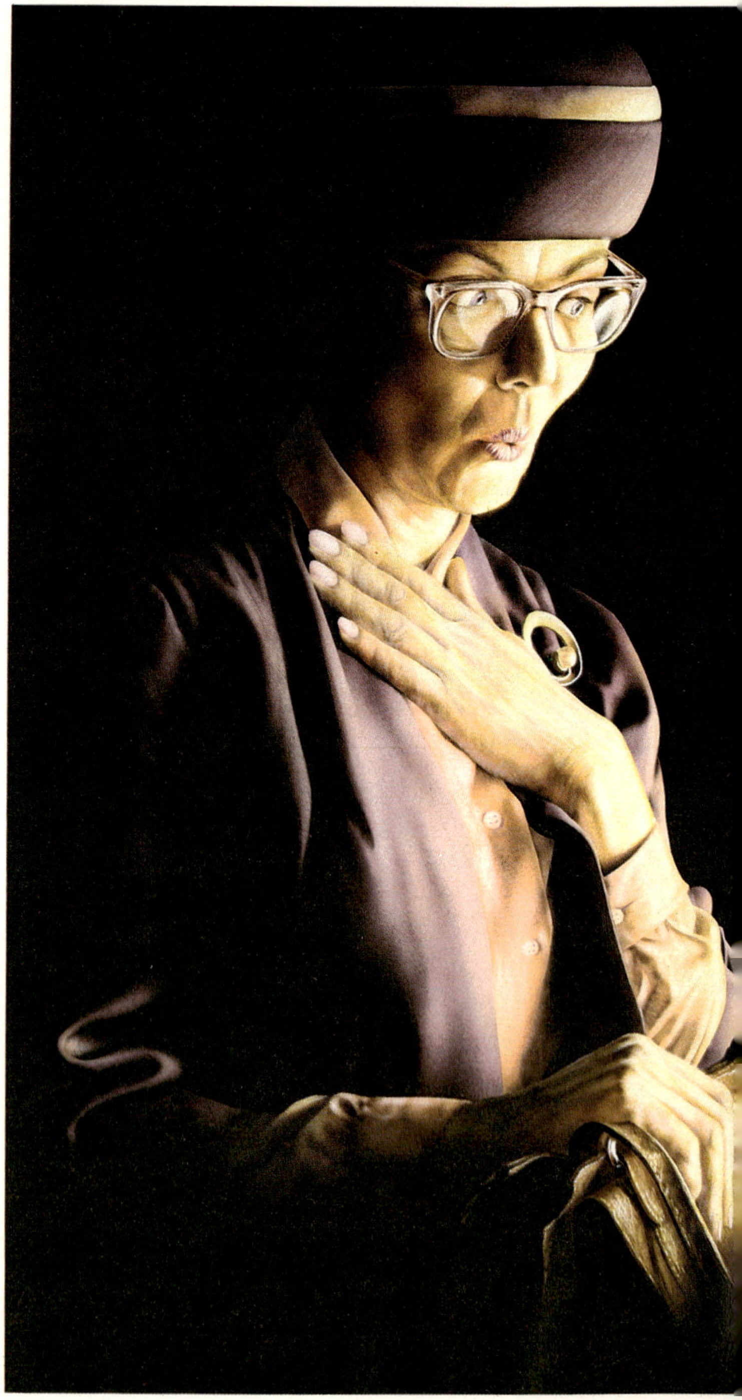

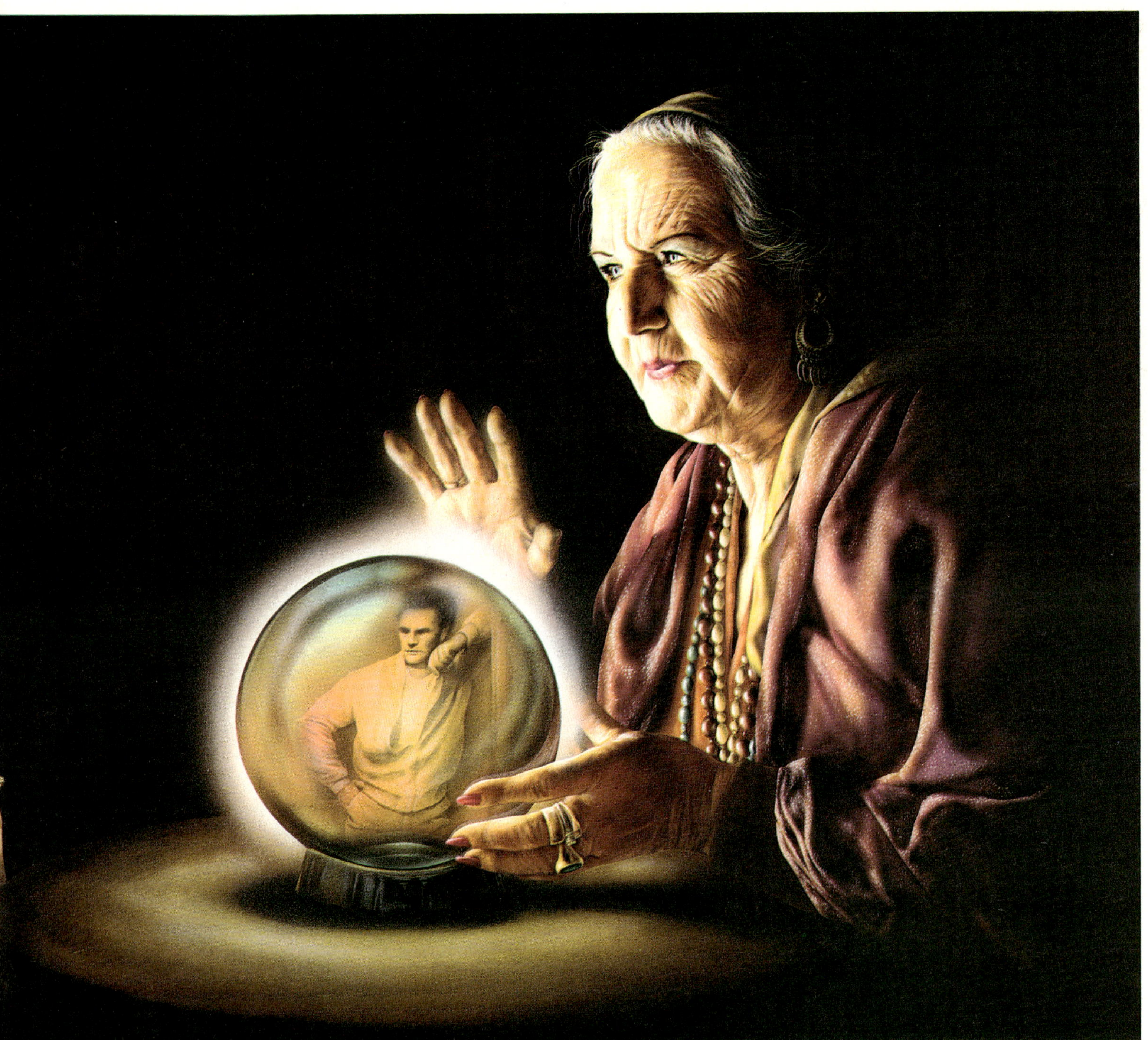

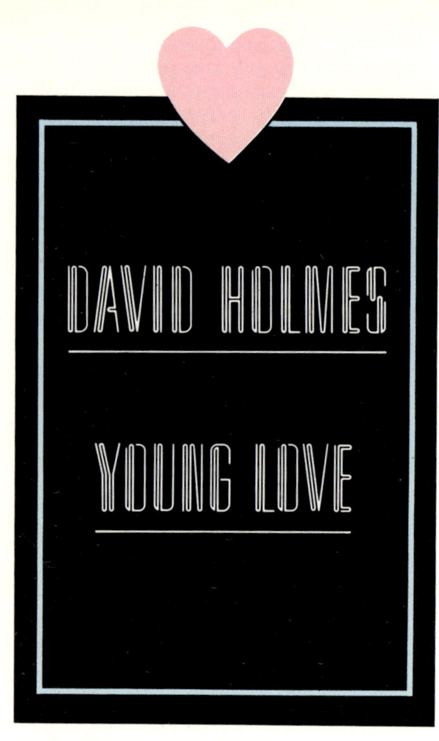
DAVID HOLMES
YOUNG LOVE

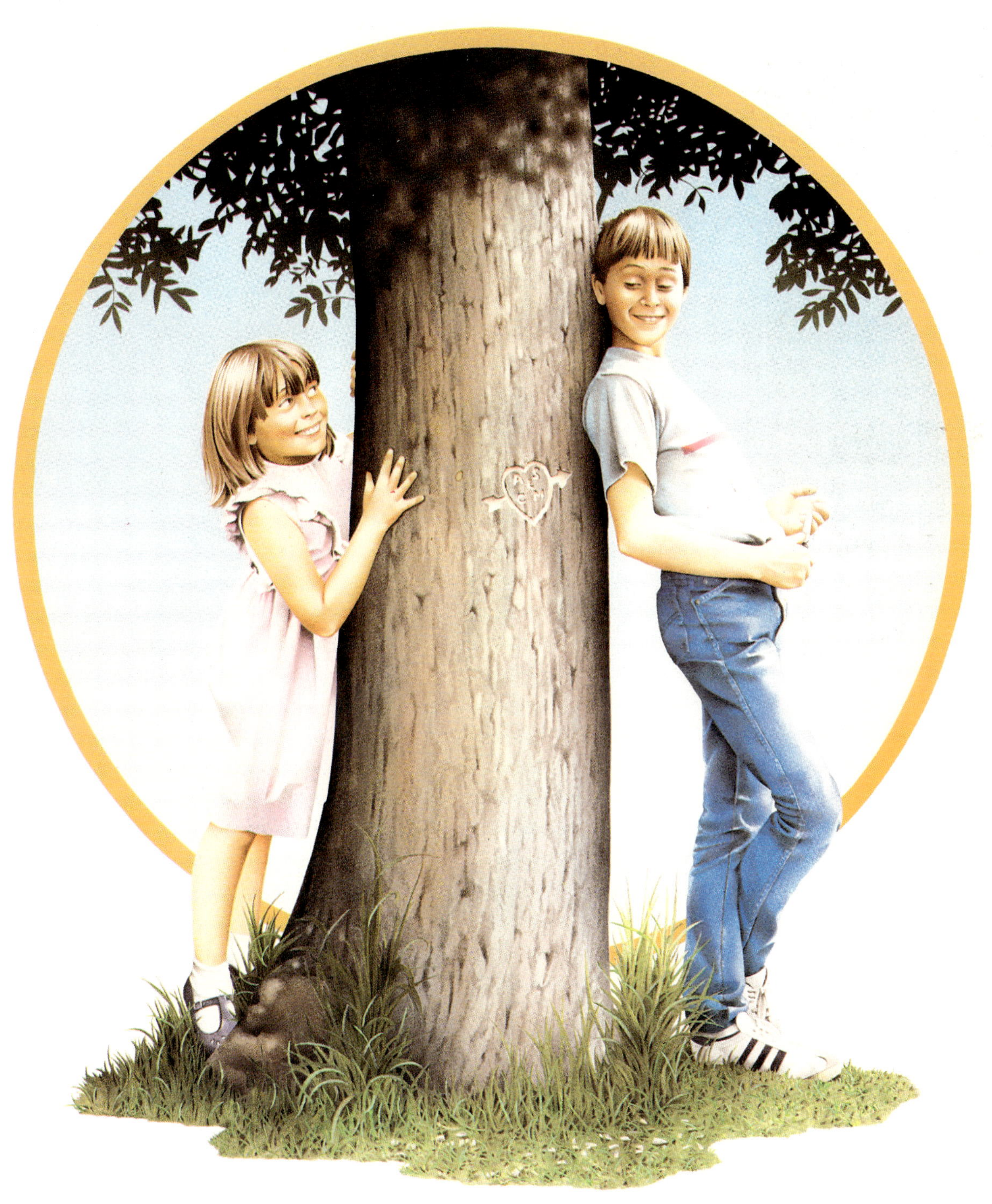

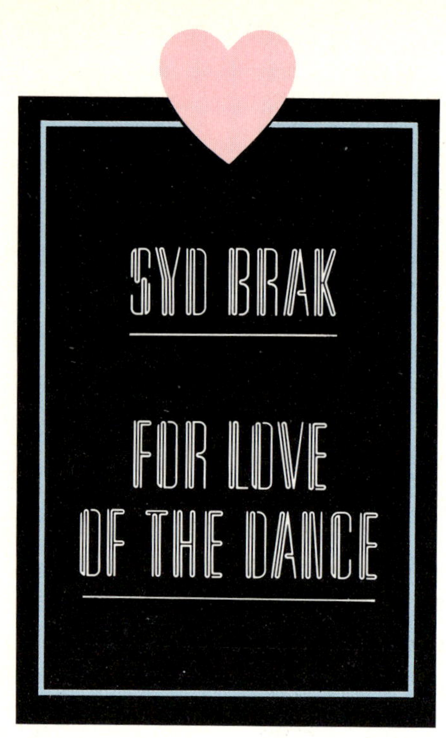
SYD BRAK
FOR LOVE
OF THE DANCE

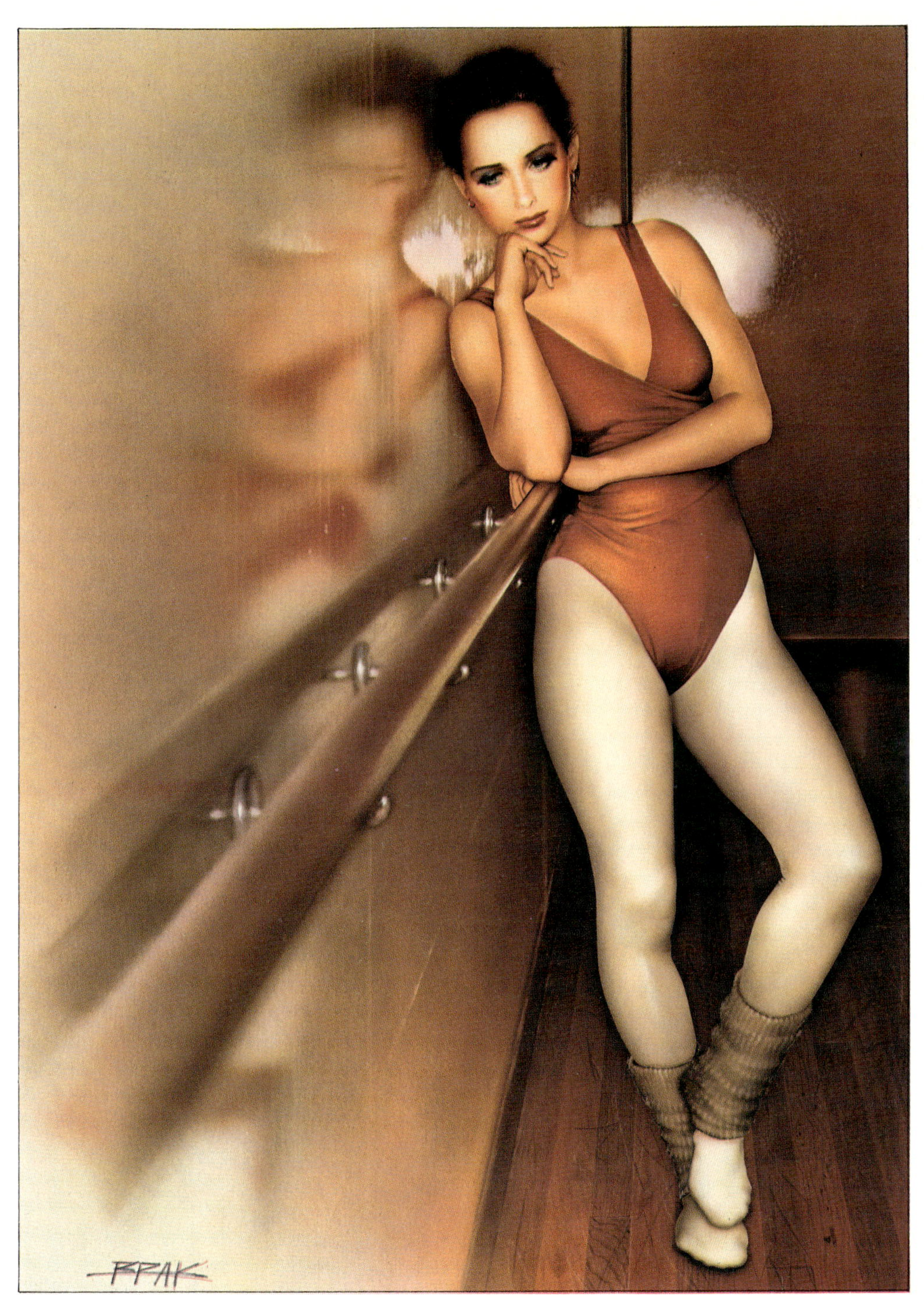
BRAK

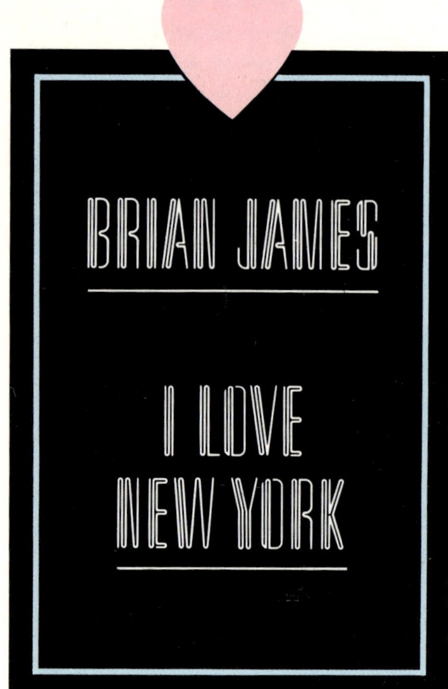
BRIAN JAMES
I LOVE
NEW YORK

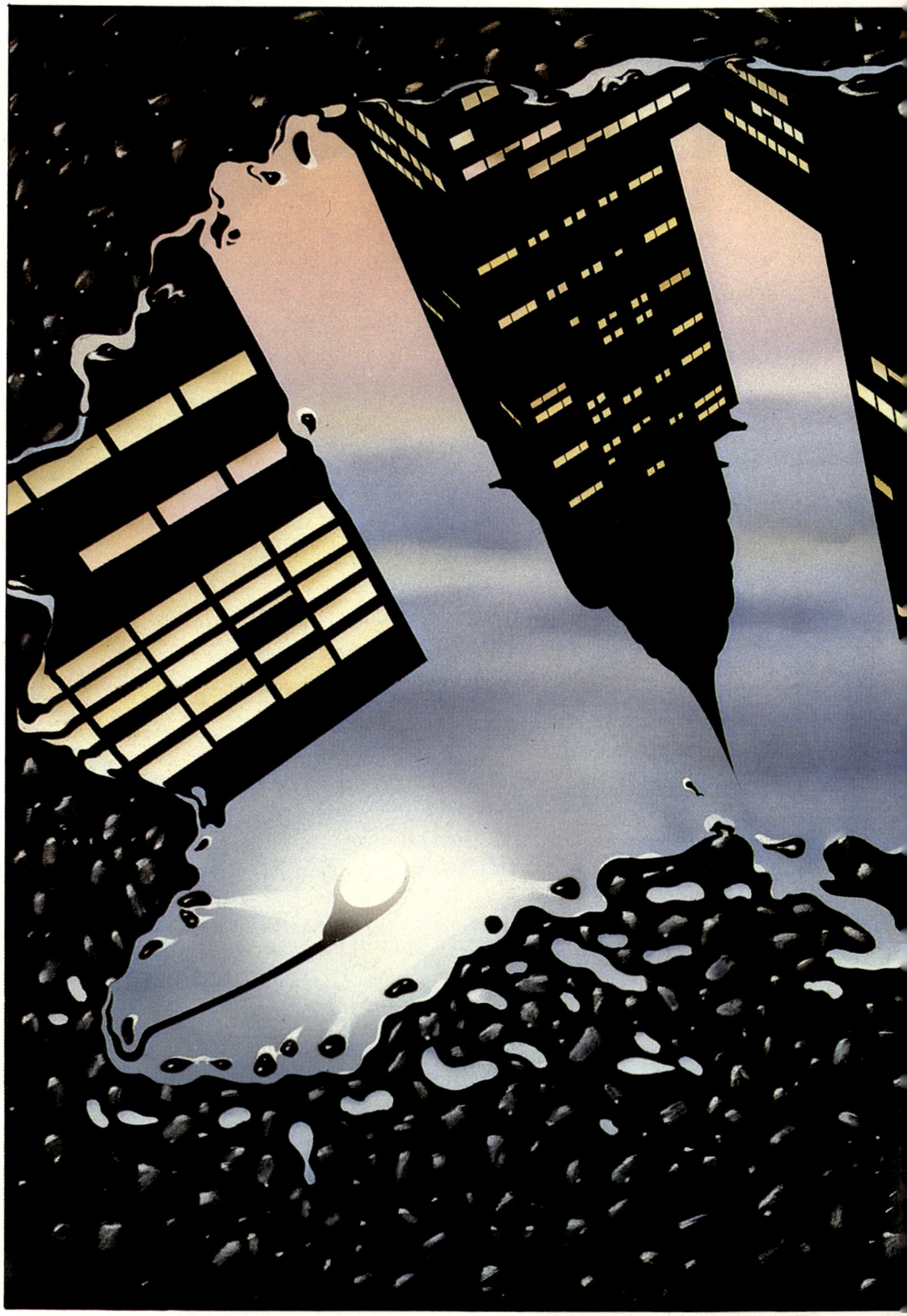

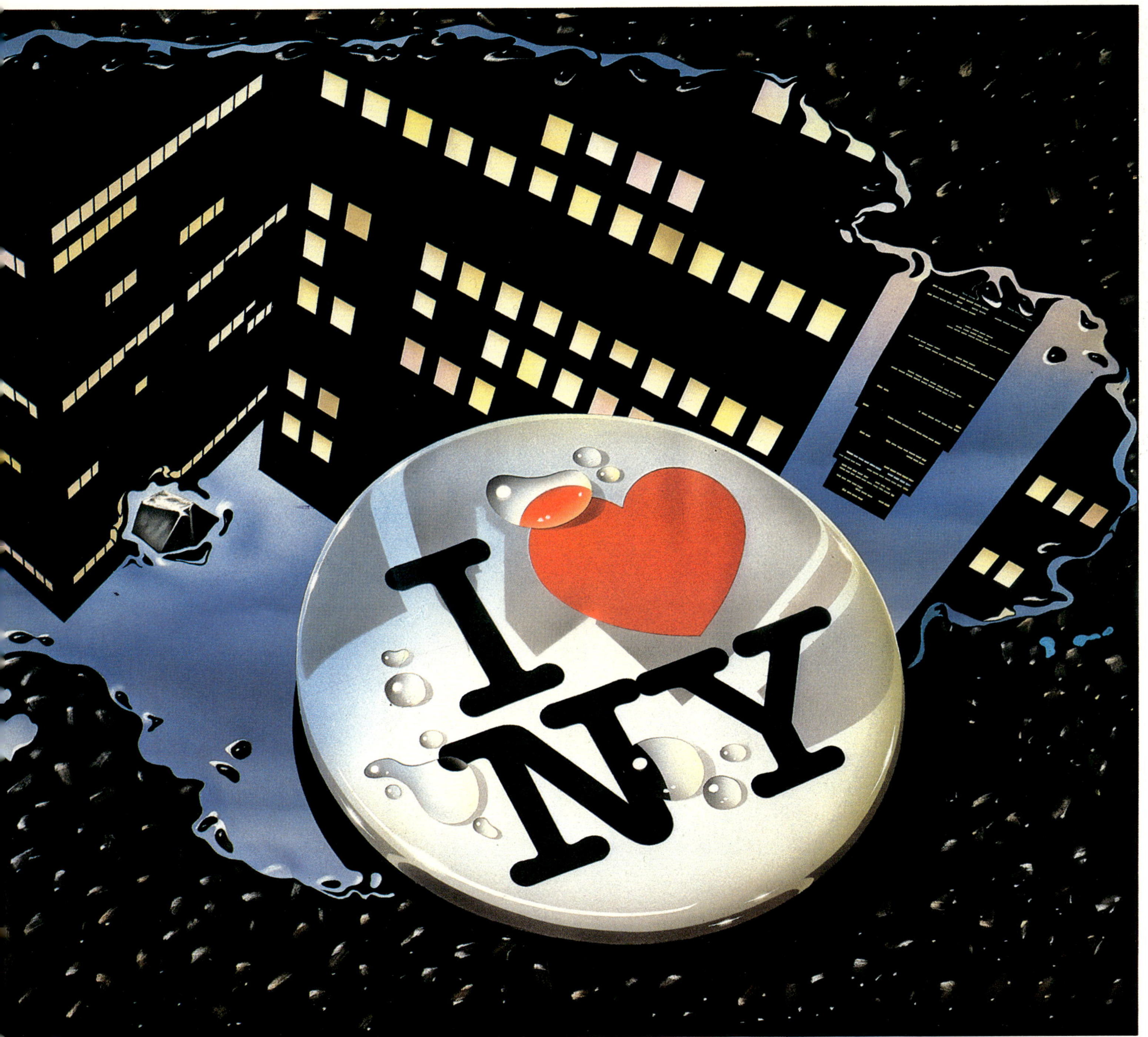
I NY

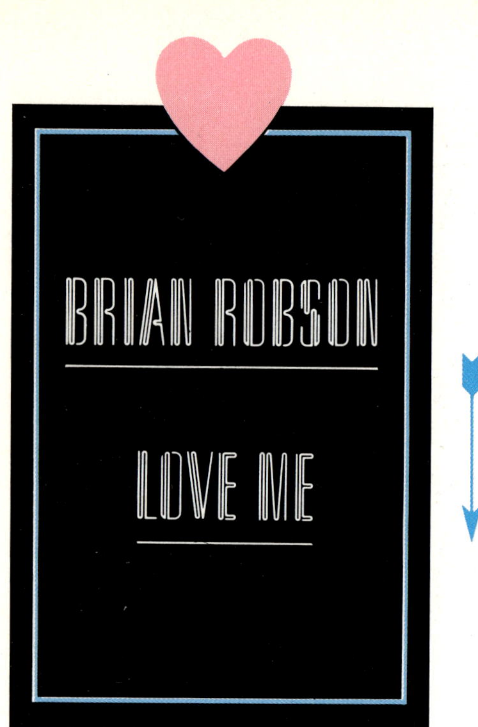
BRIAN ROBSON
LOVE ME

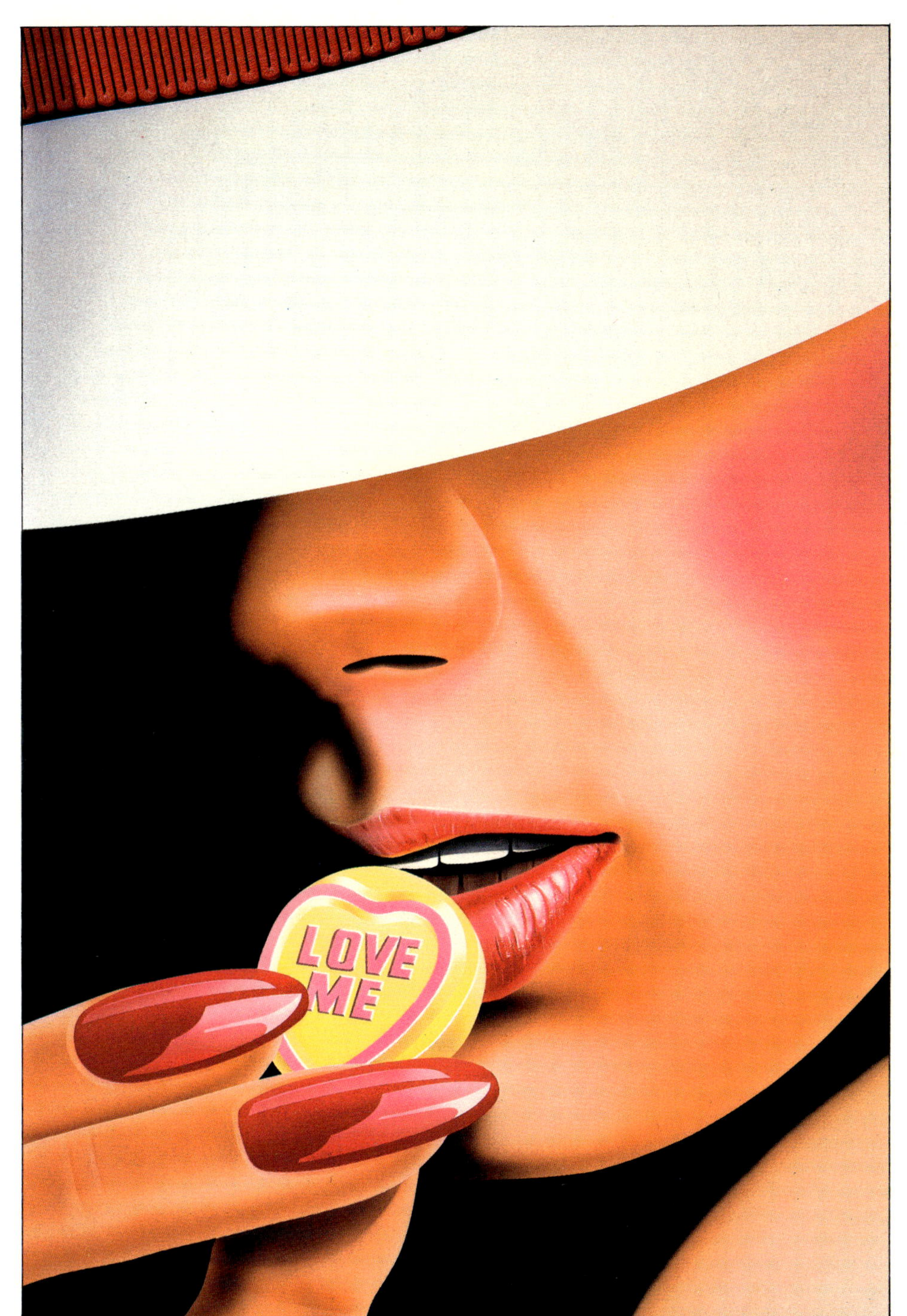
LOVE
ME

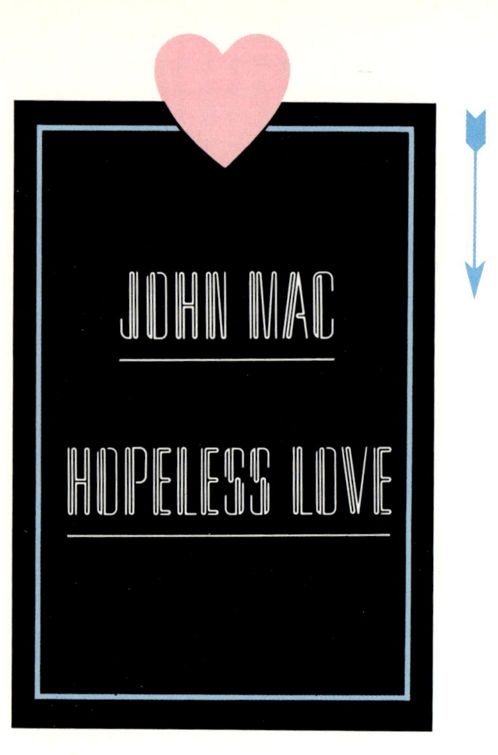
JOHN MAC
HOPELESS LOVE

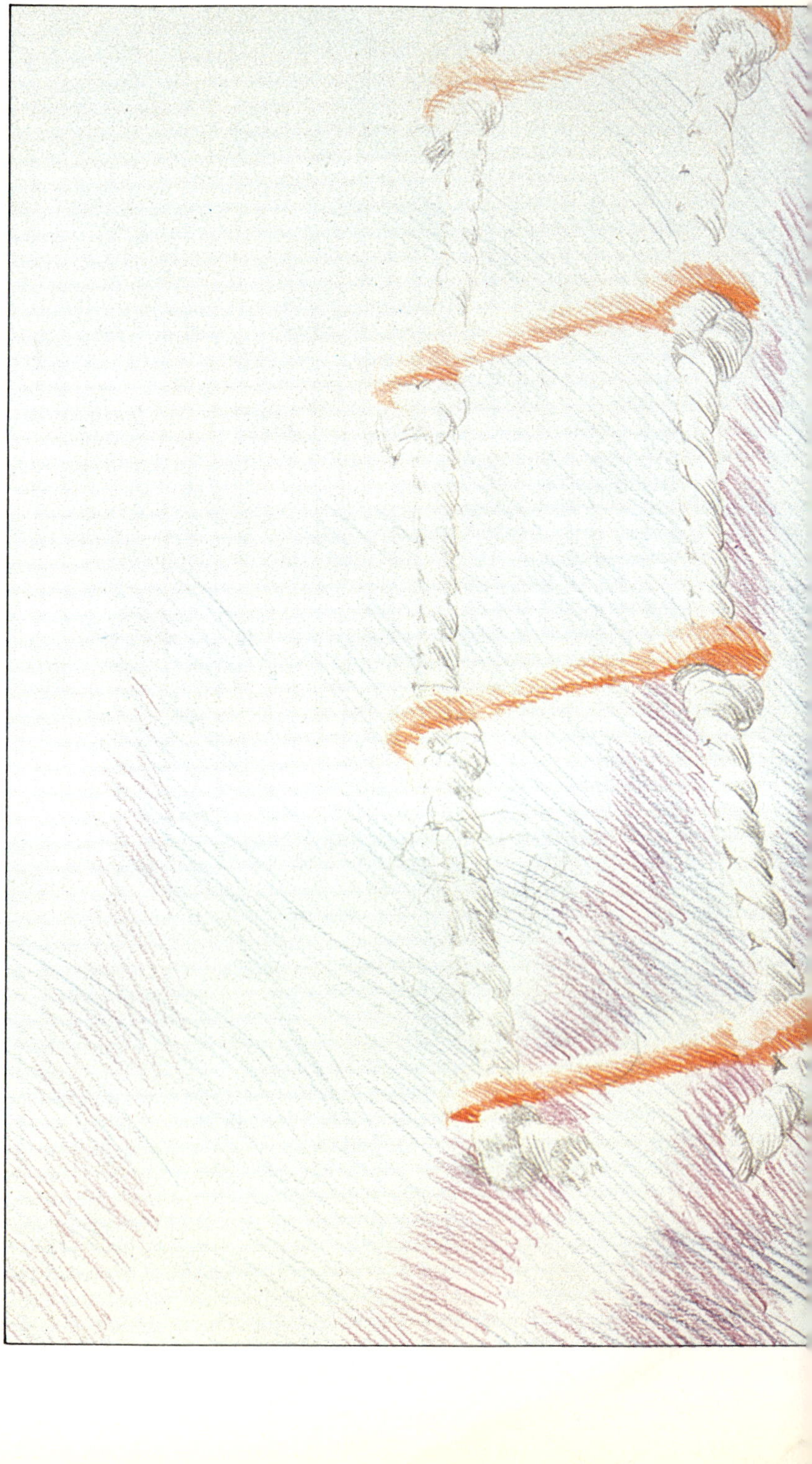

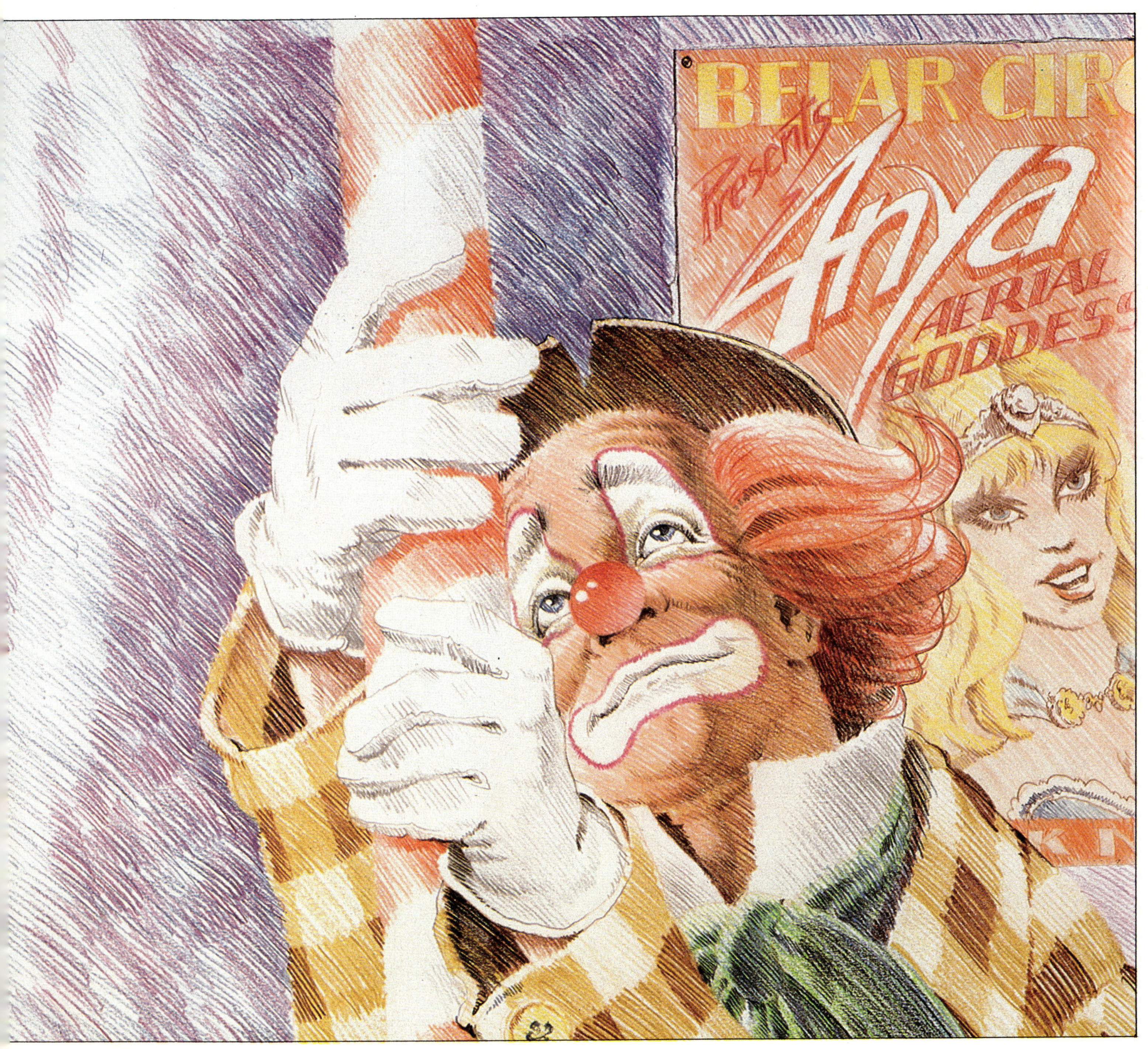

BELAR CIRC
Presents
Anya
AERIAL
GODDES

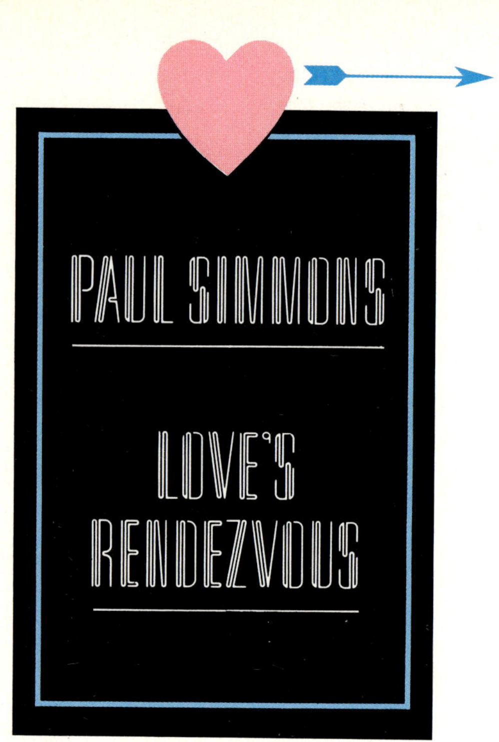
PAUL SIMMONS
LOVE'S
RENDEZVOUS

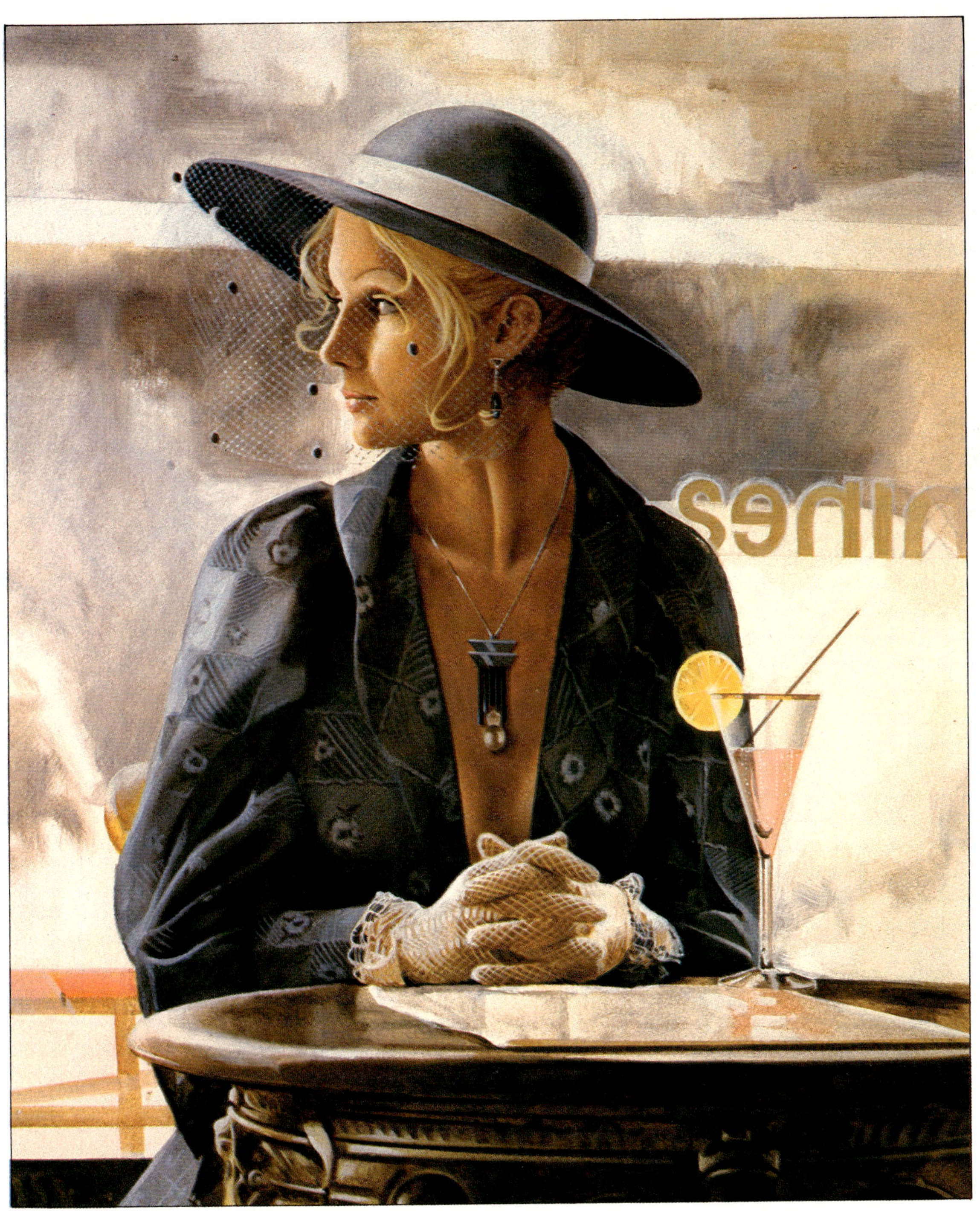

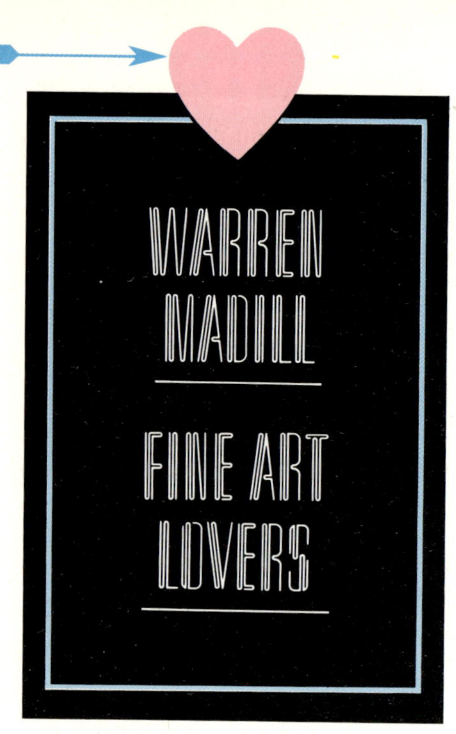
WARREN
MADILL
FINE ART
LOVERS

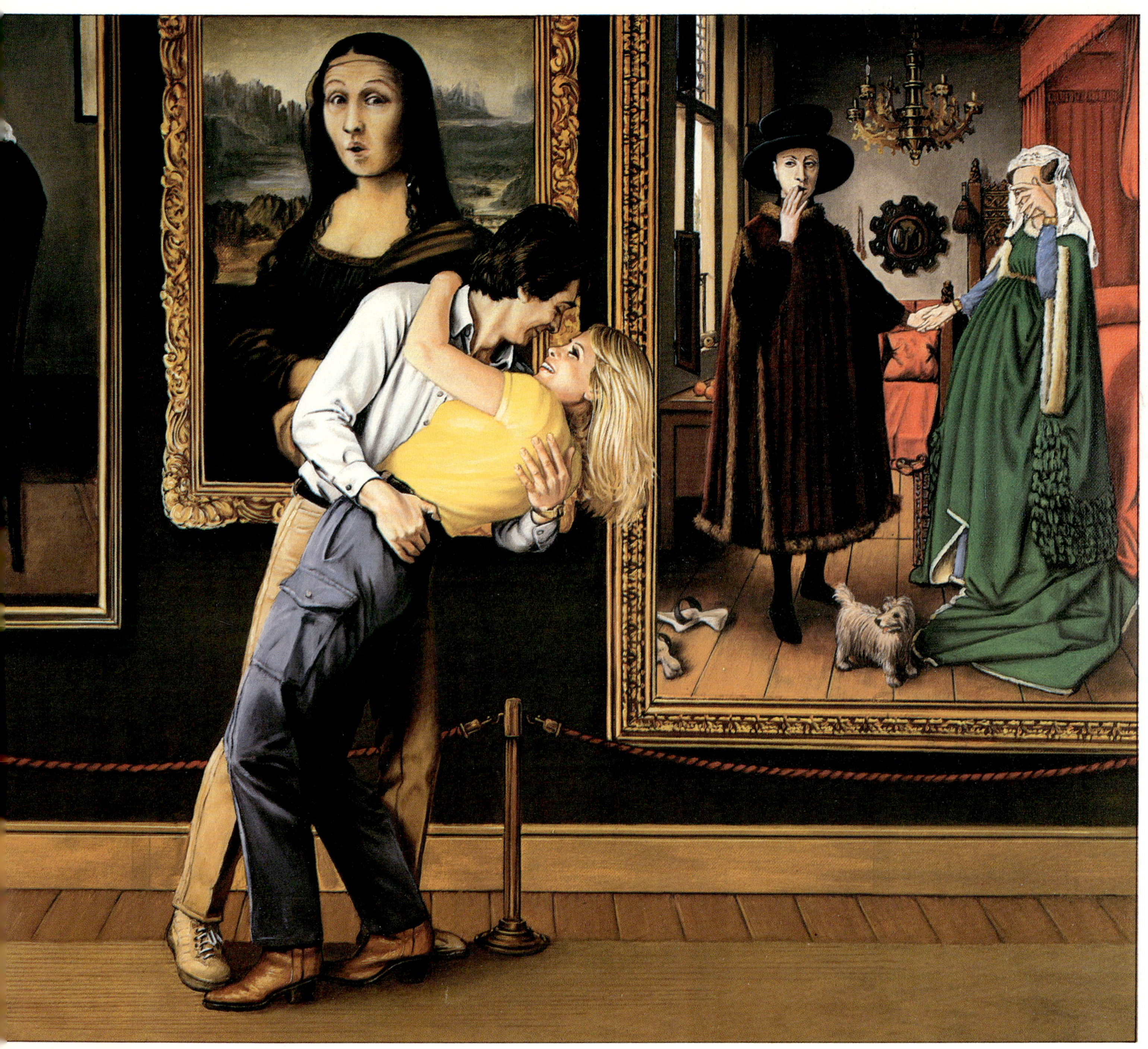

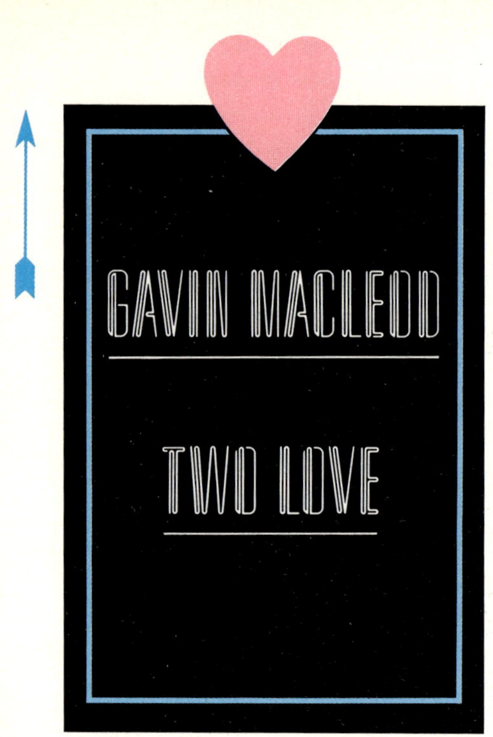
GAVIN MACLEOD
TWO LOVE

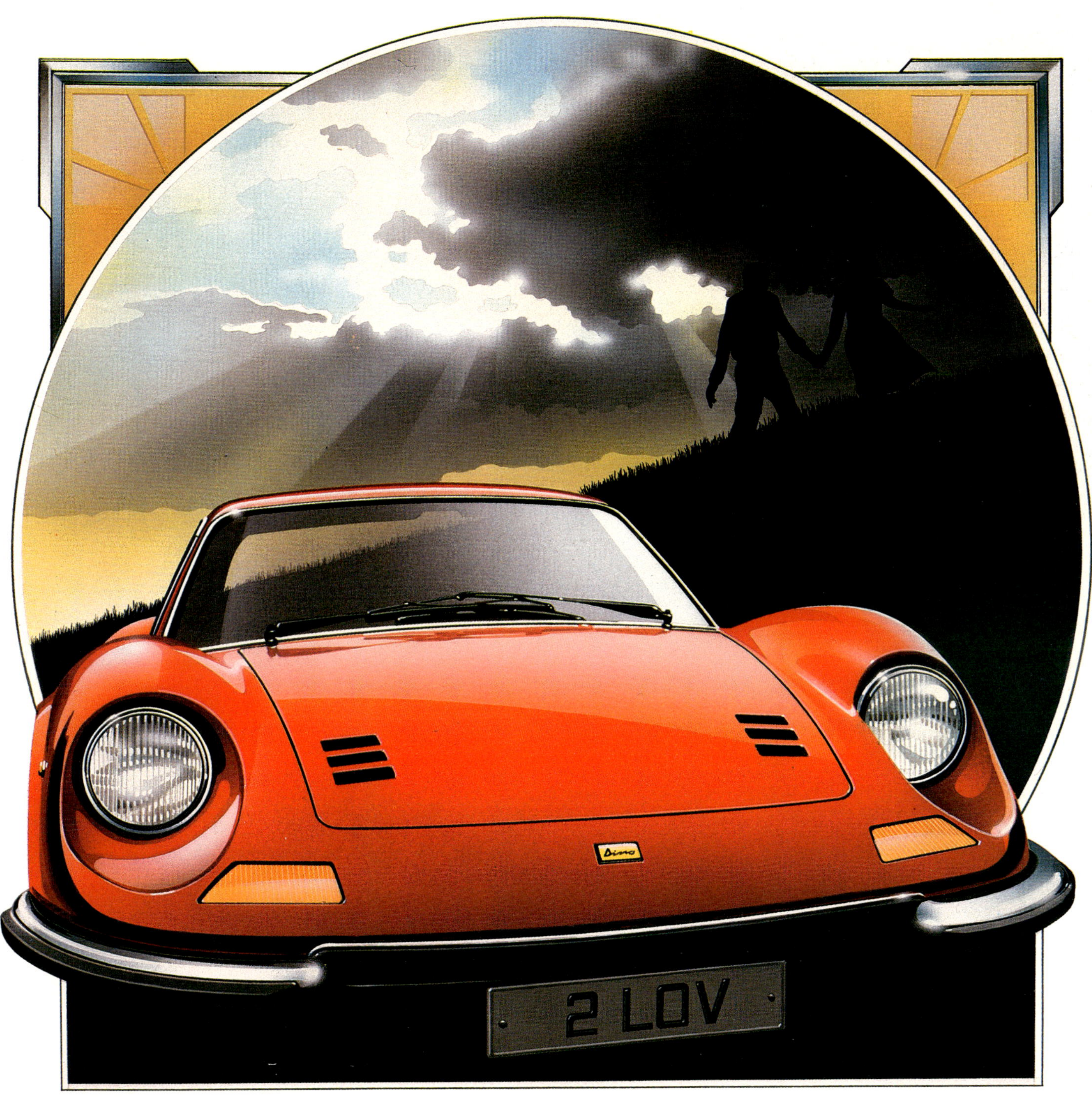
2 LOV

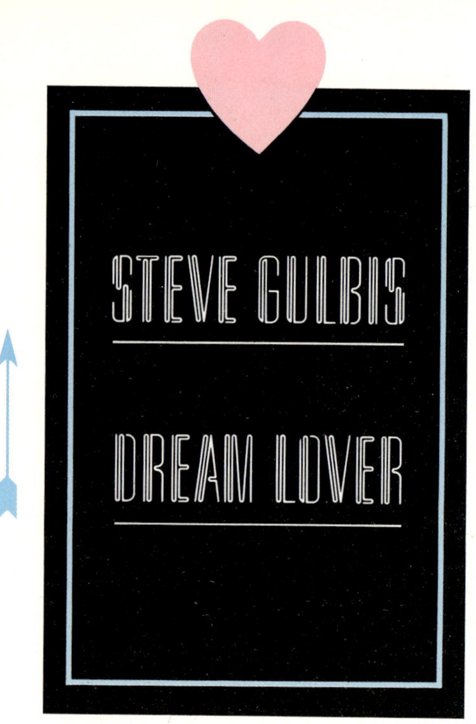
STEVE GULBIS
DREAM LOVER

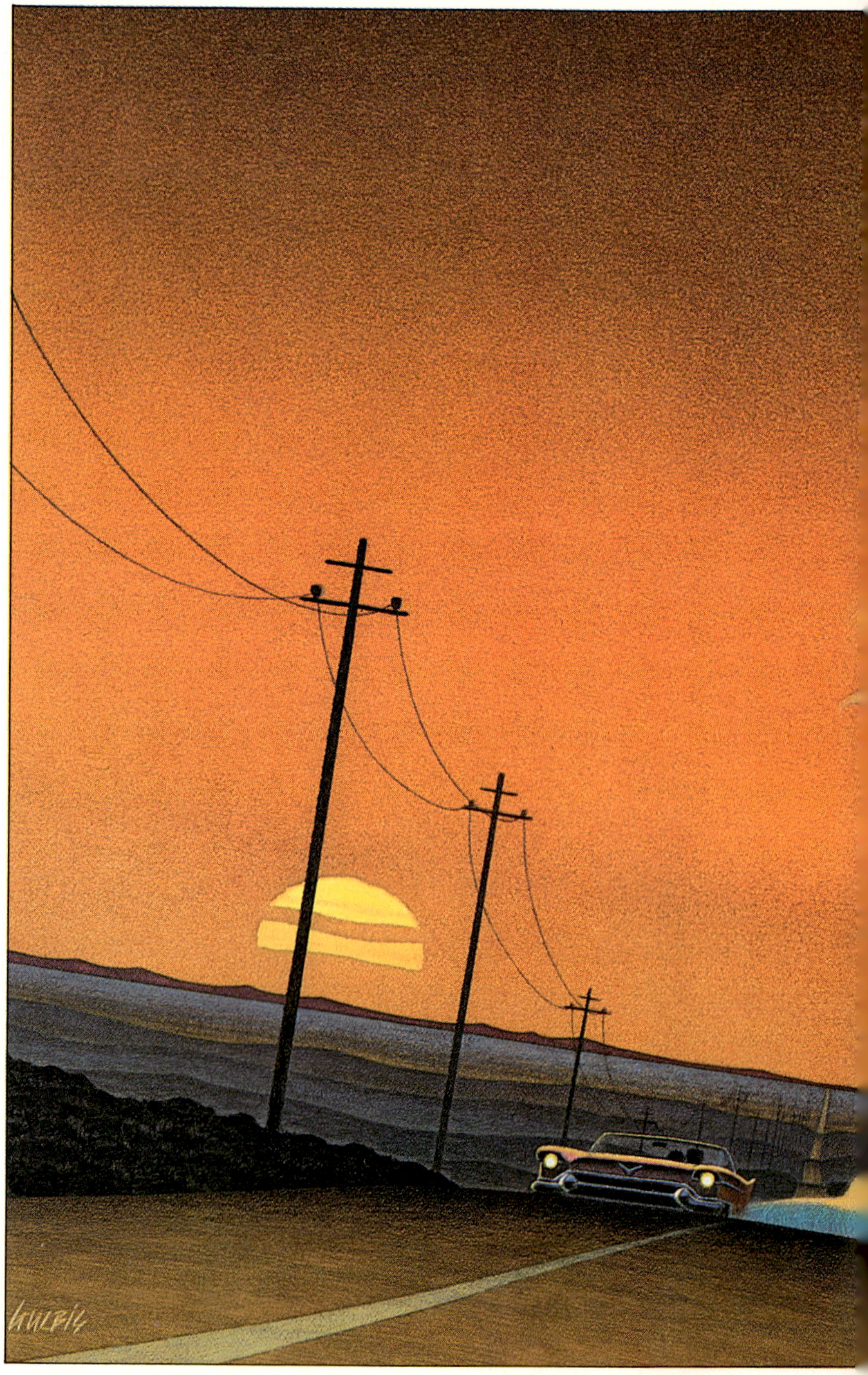

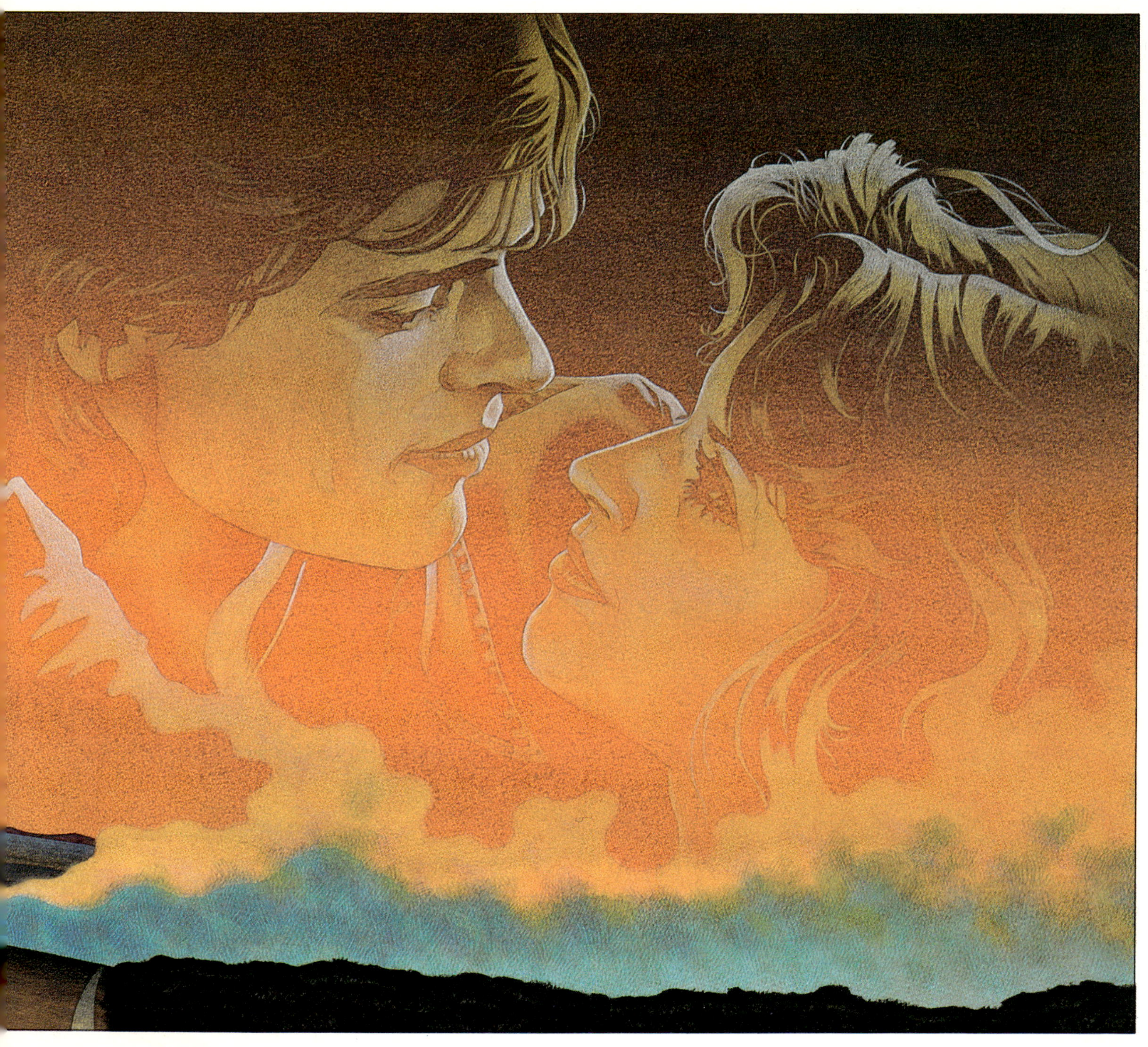

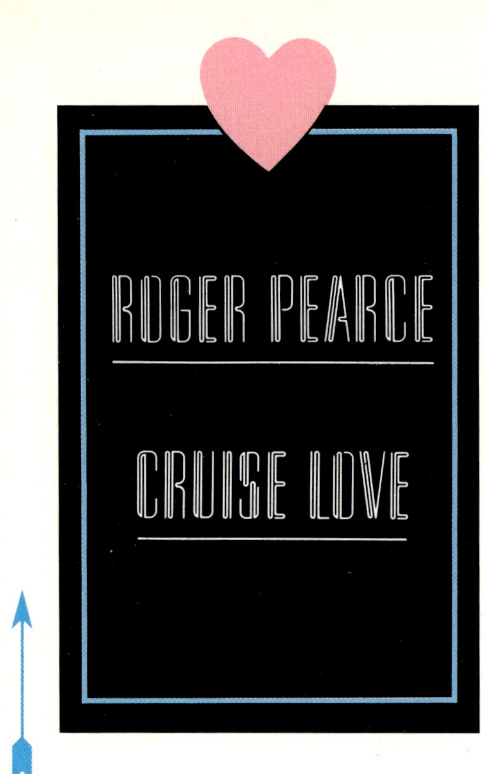
ROGER PEARCE
CRUISE LOVE

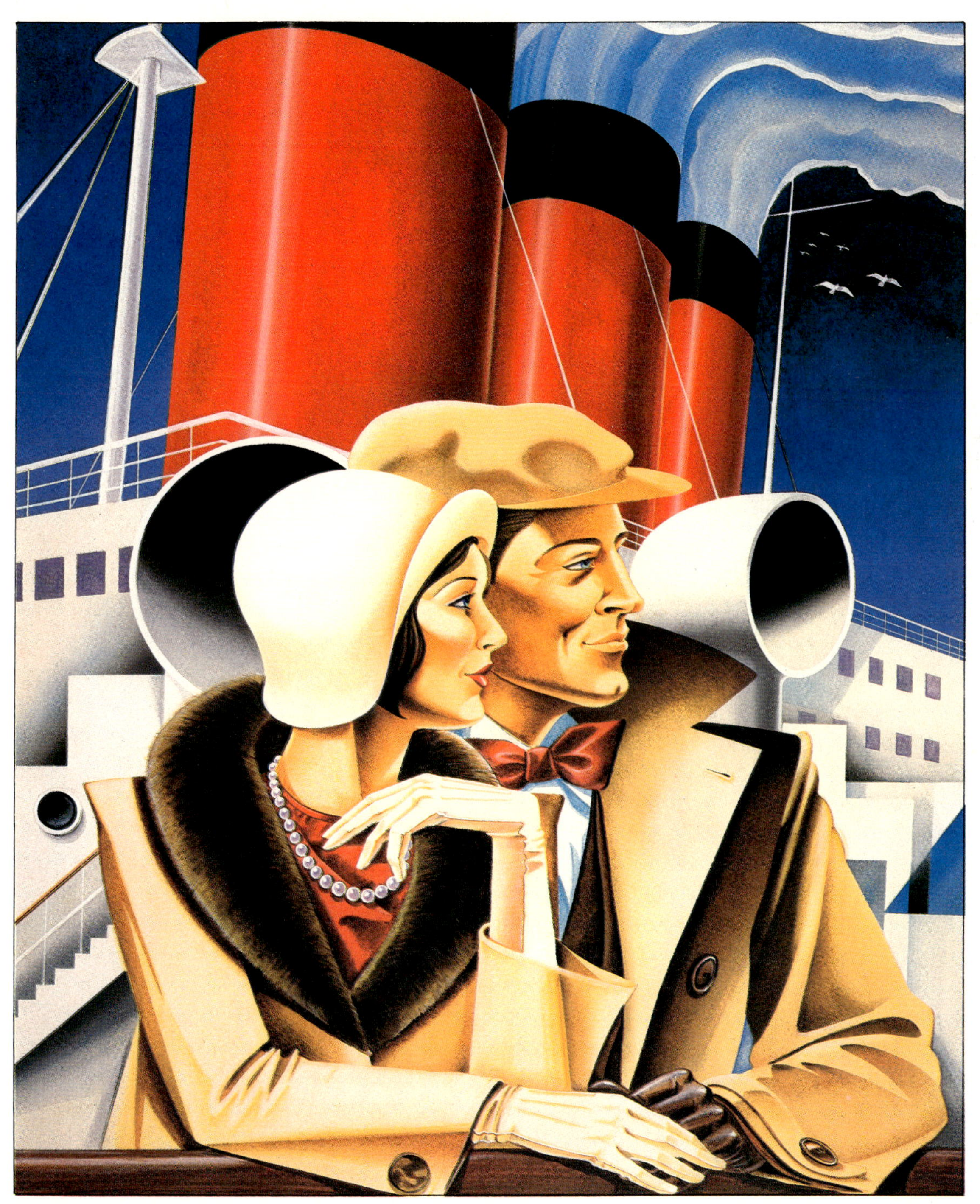

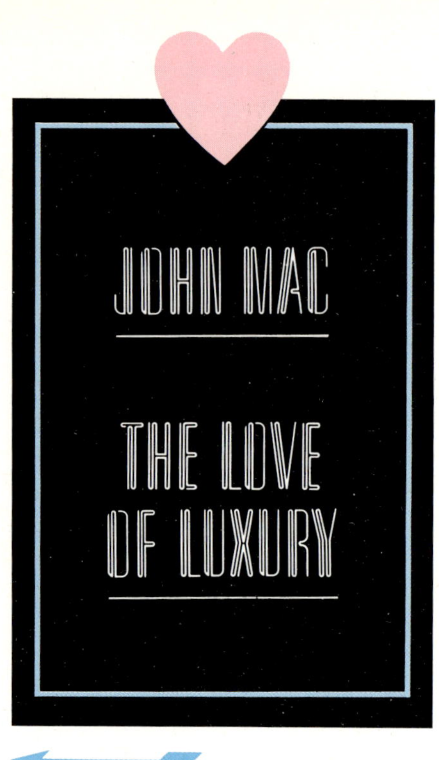
JOHN MAC
THE LOVE
OF LUXURY

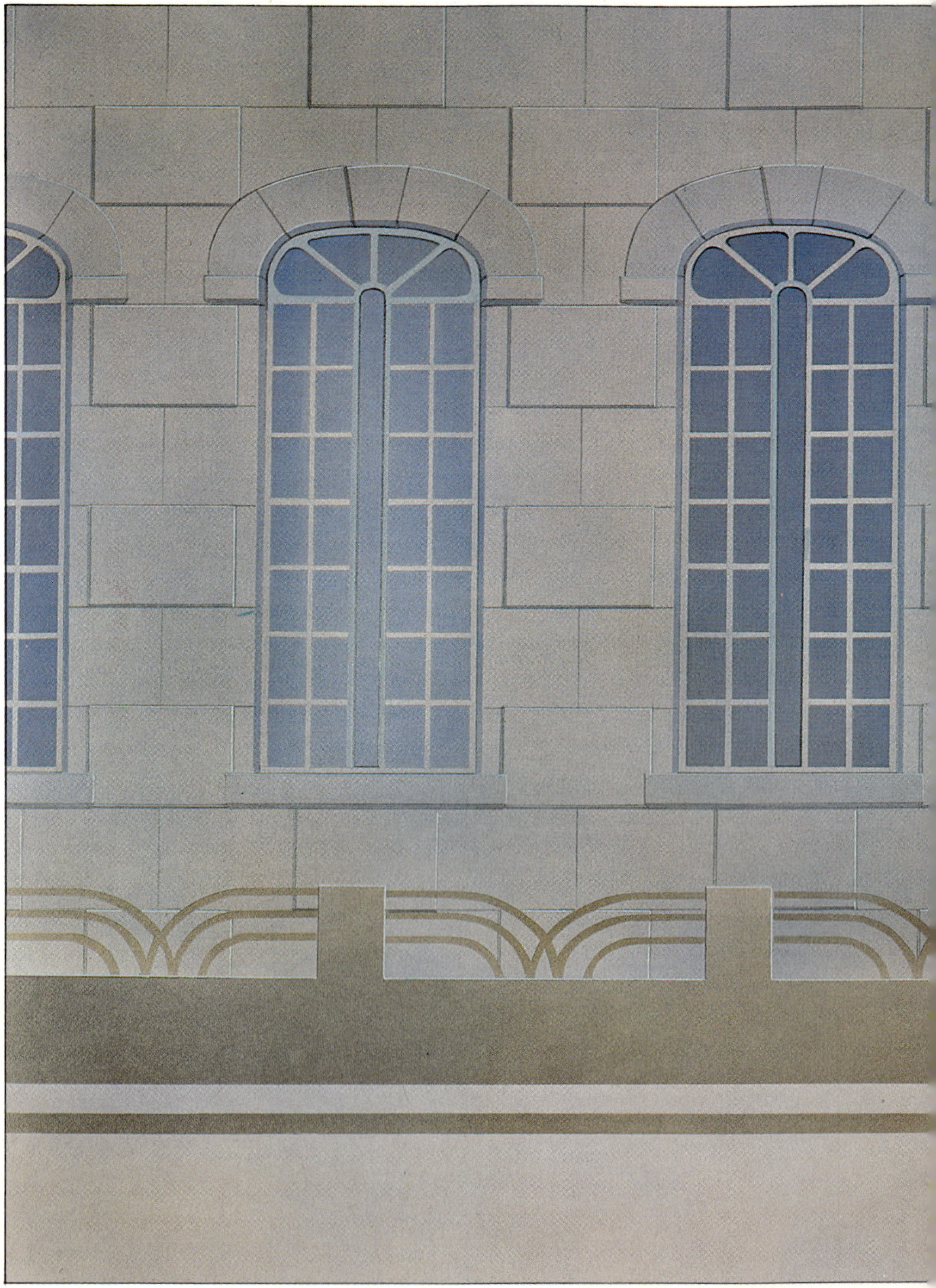

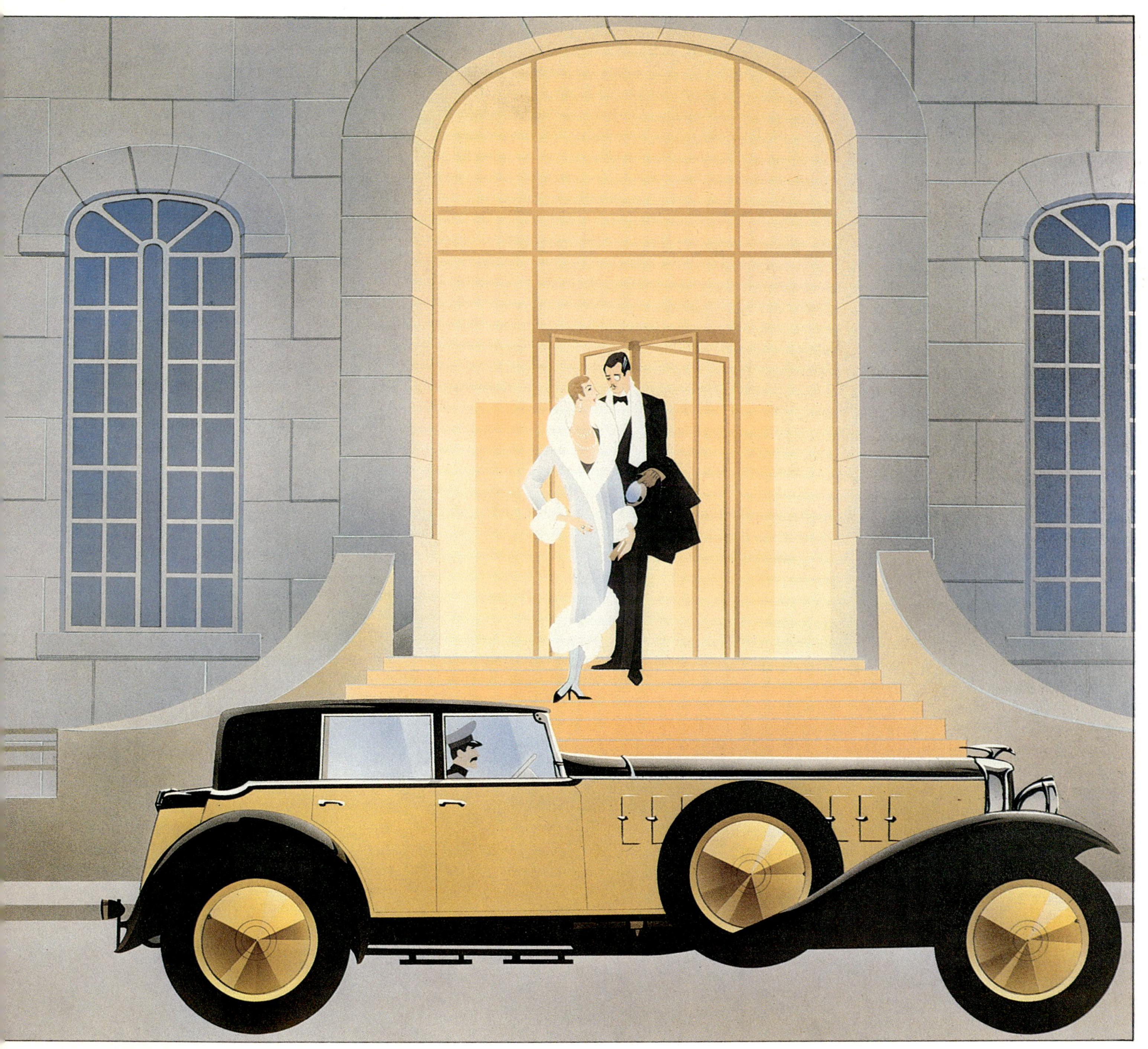

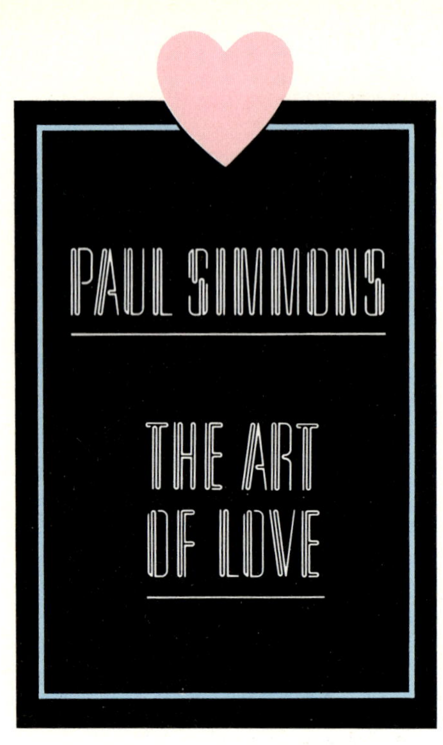
PAUL SIMMONS
THE ART
OF LOVE

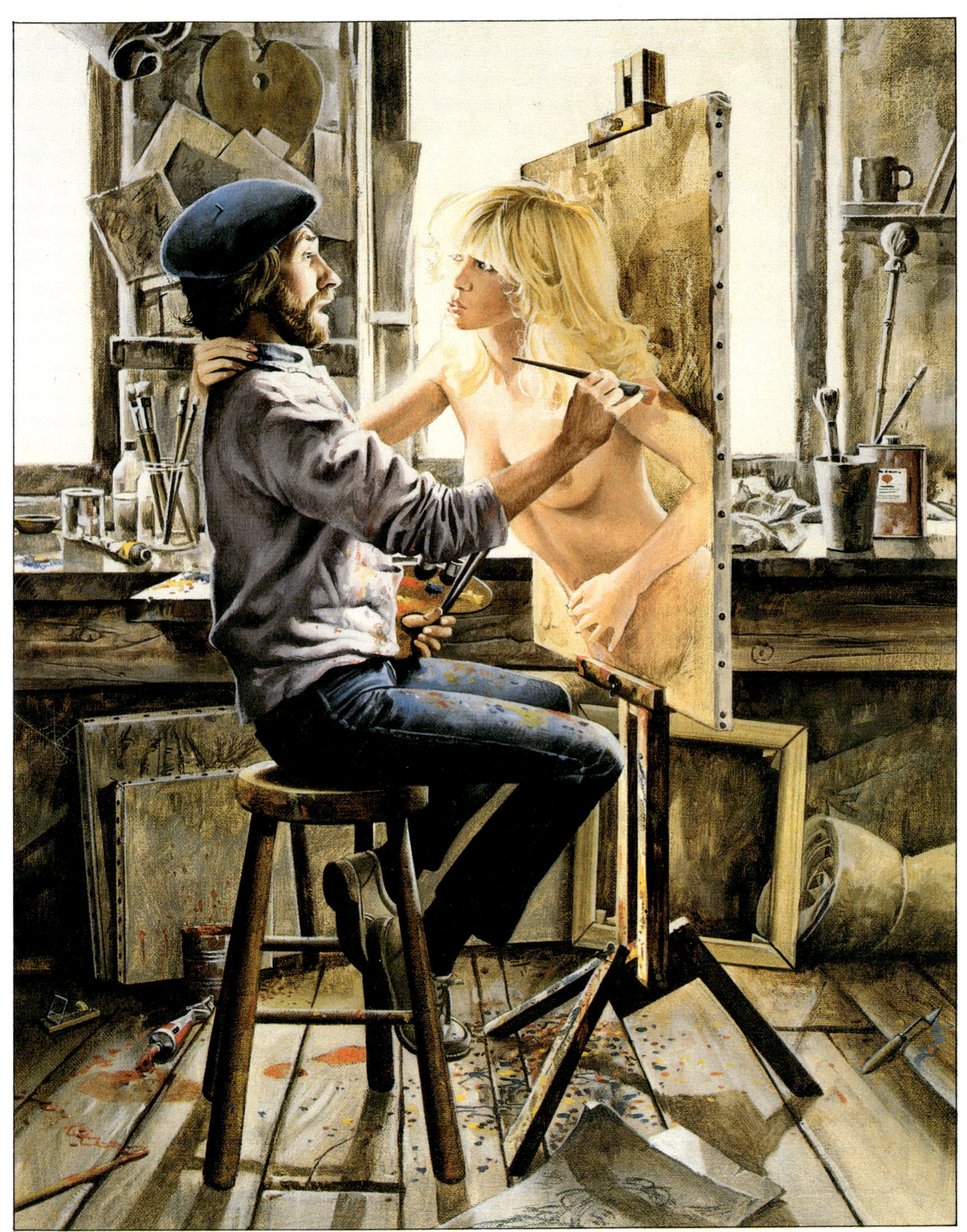

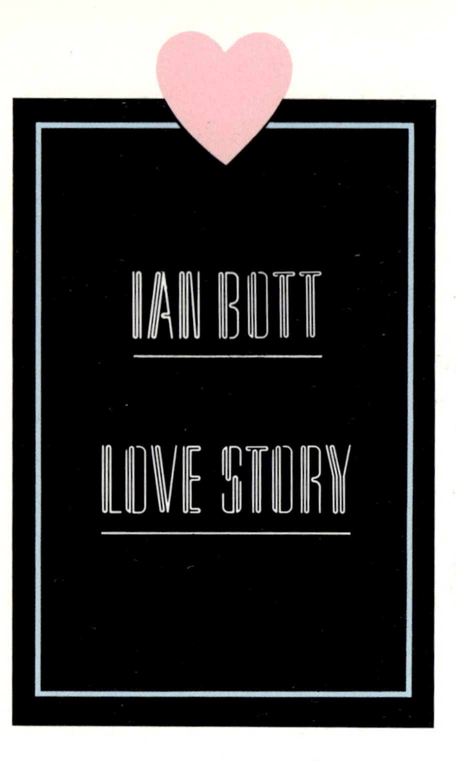
IAN BOTT
LOVE STORY

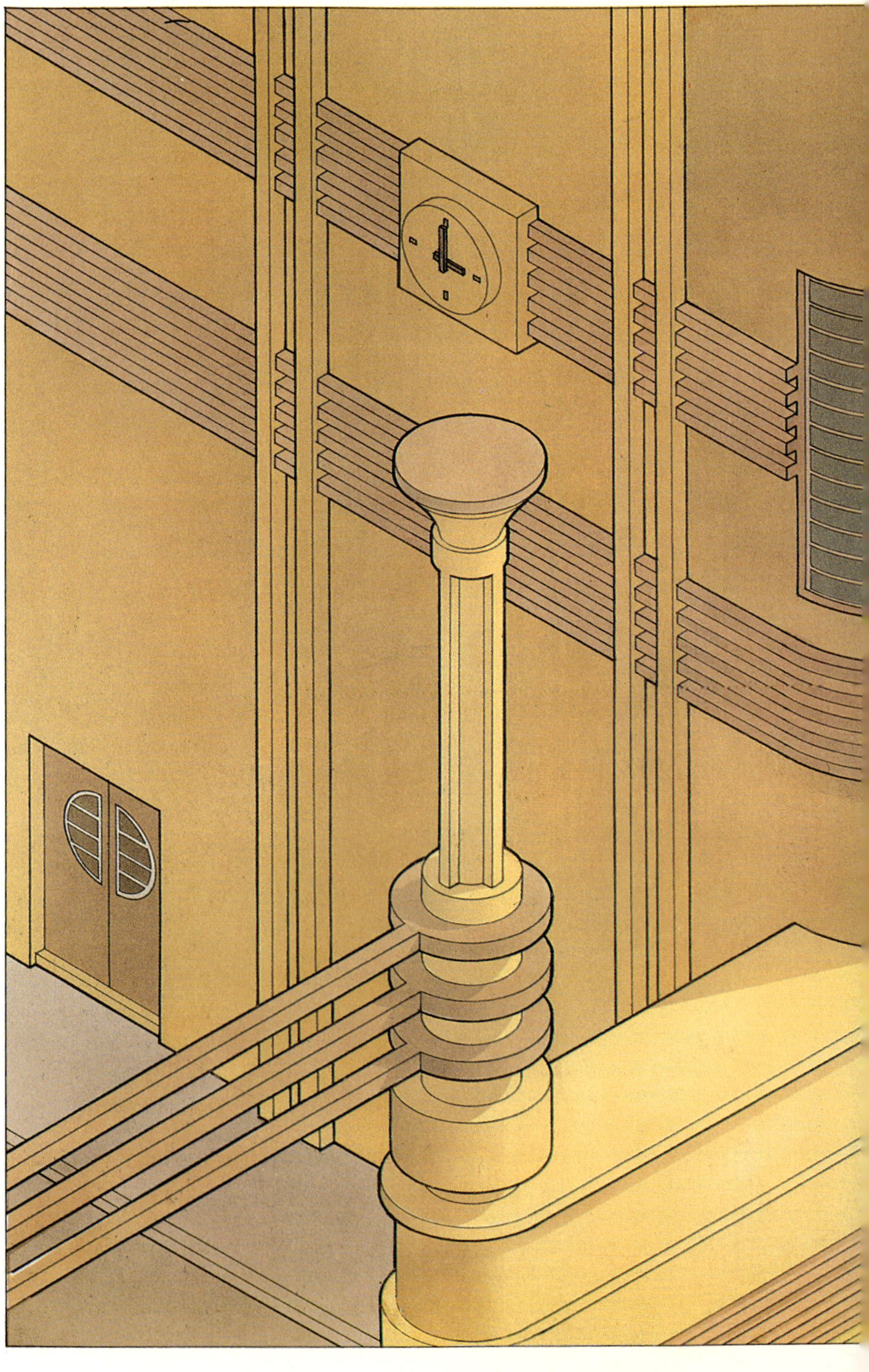

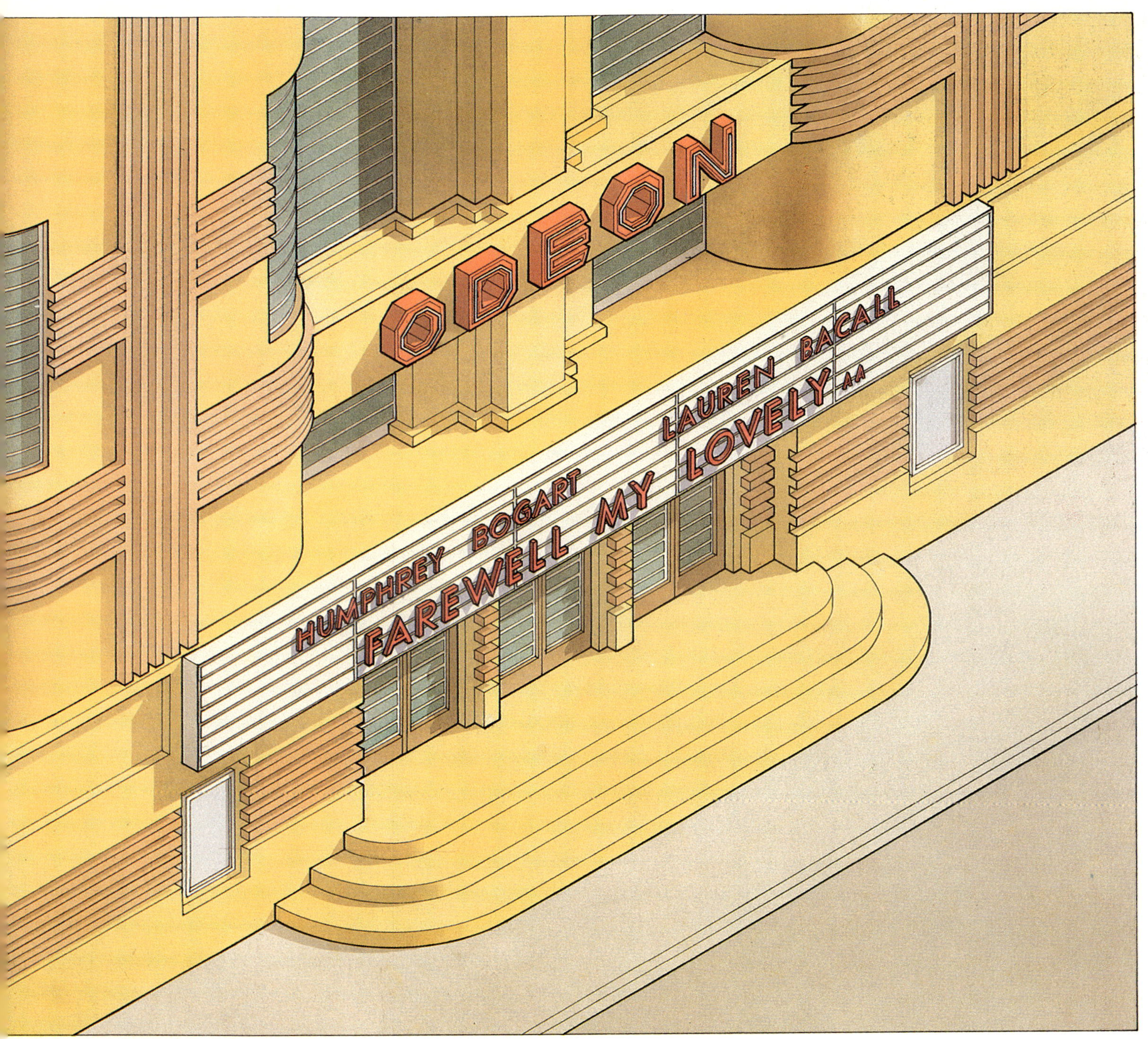
ODEON
HUMPHREY BOGART LAUREN BACALL
FAREWELL MY LOVELY AA

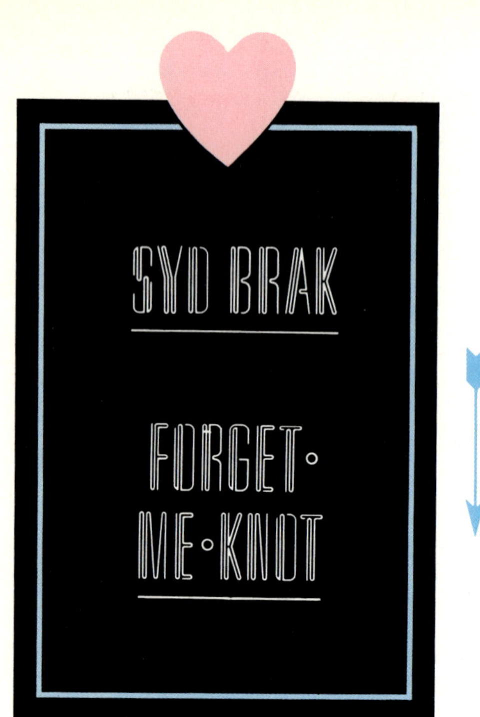
SYD BRAK
FORGET·
ME·KNOT

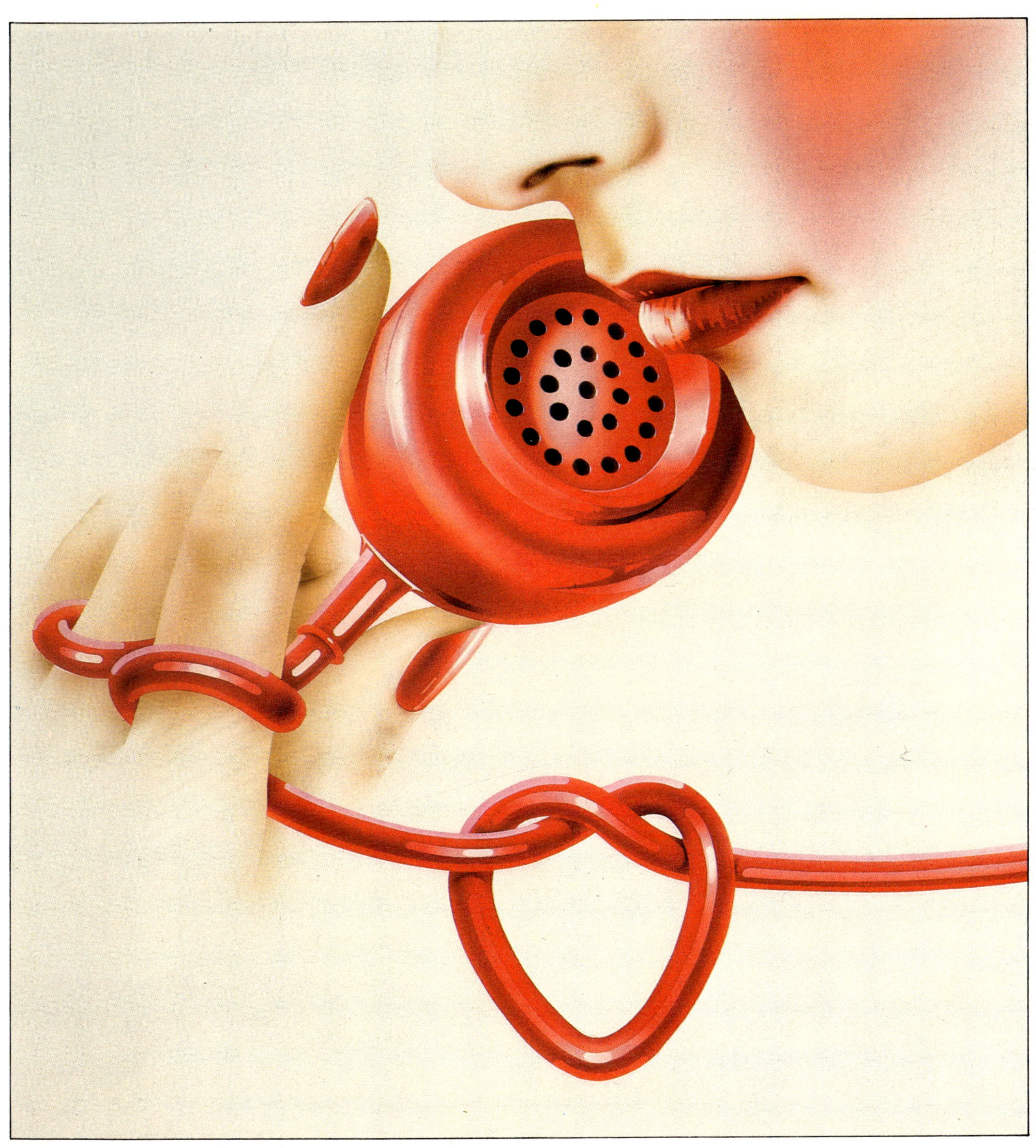

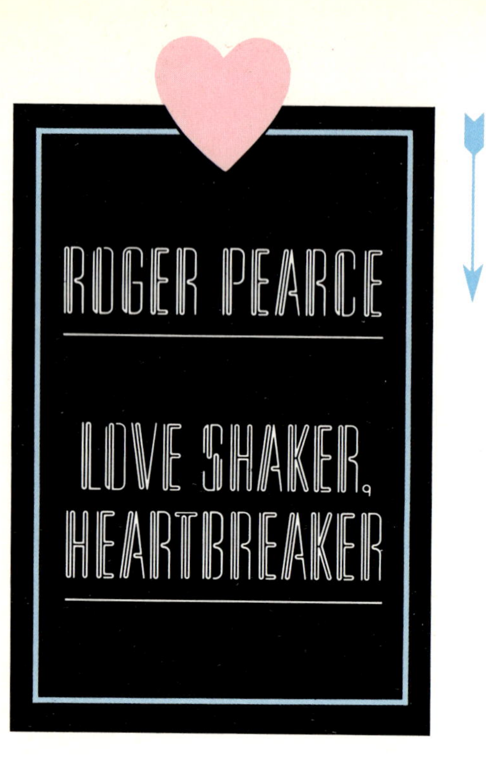
ROGER PEARCE
LOVE SHAKER, HEARTBREAKER

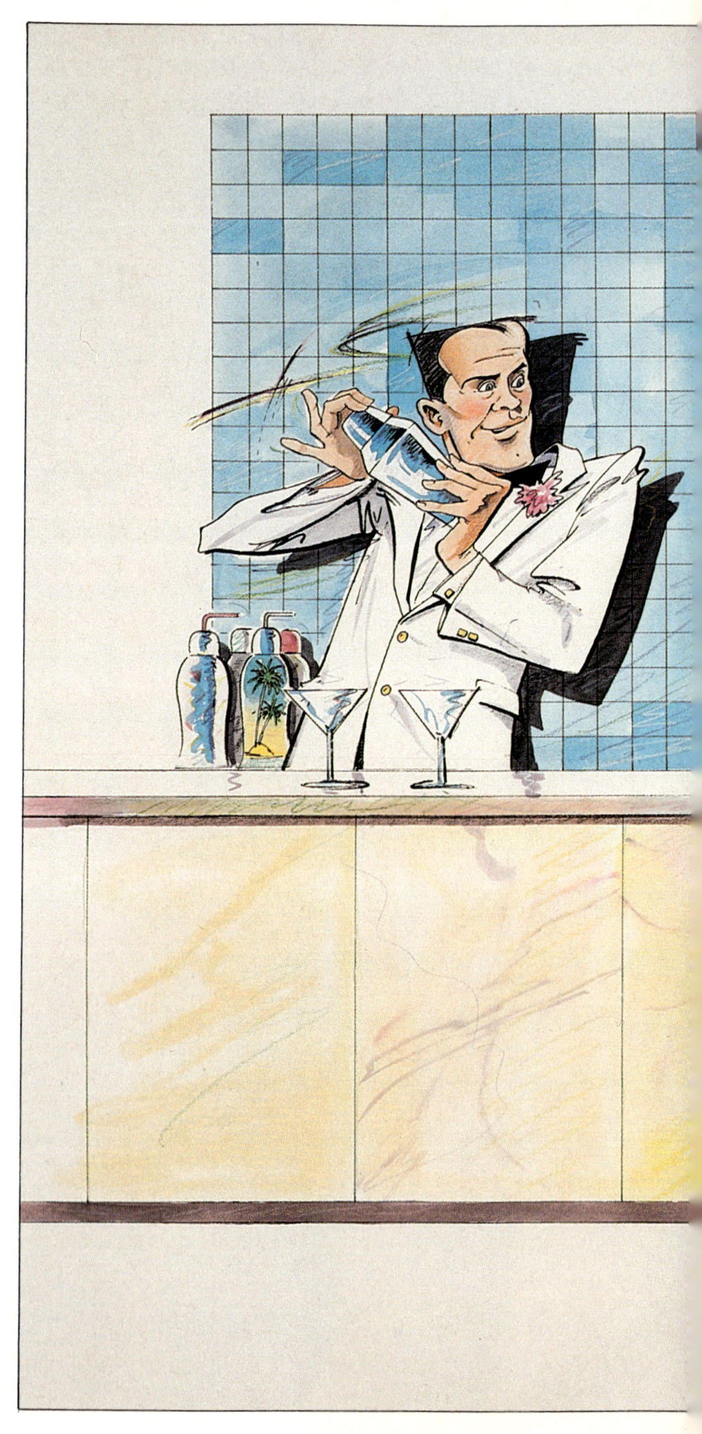

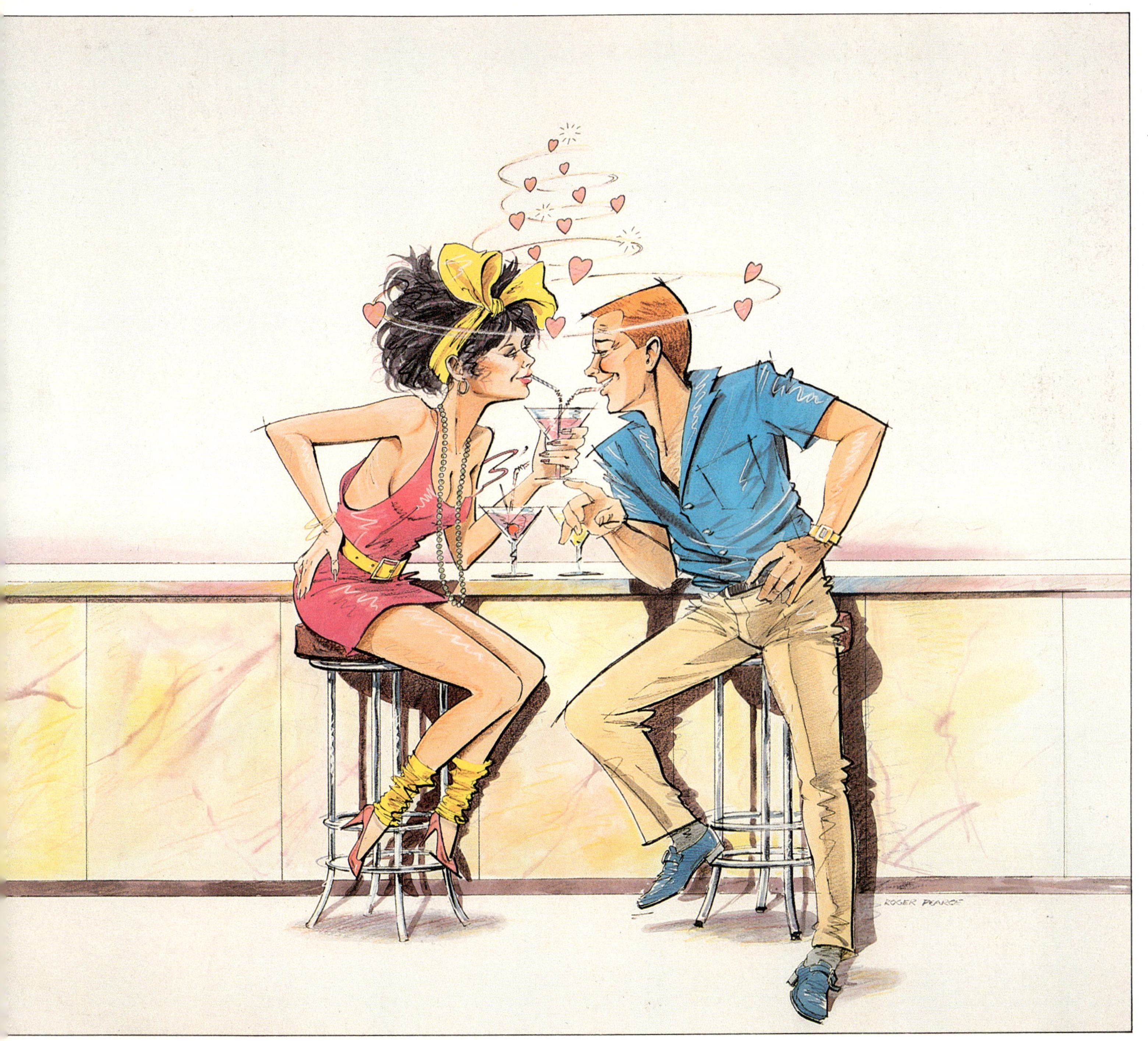
ROGER PEARCE

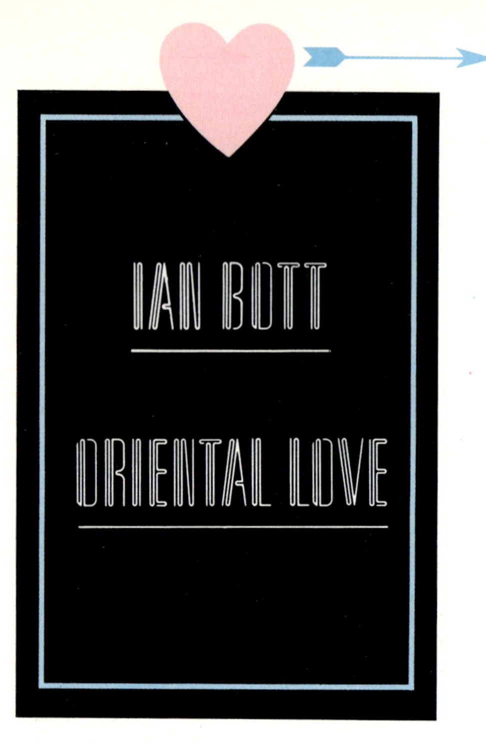
IAN BOTT
ORIENTAL LOVE

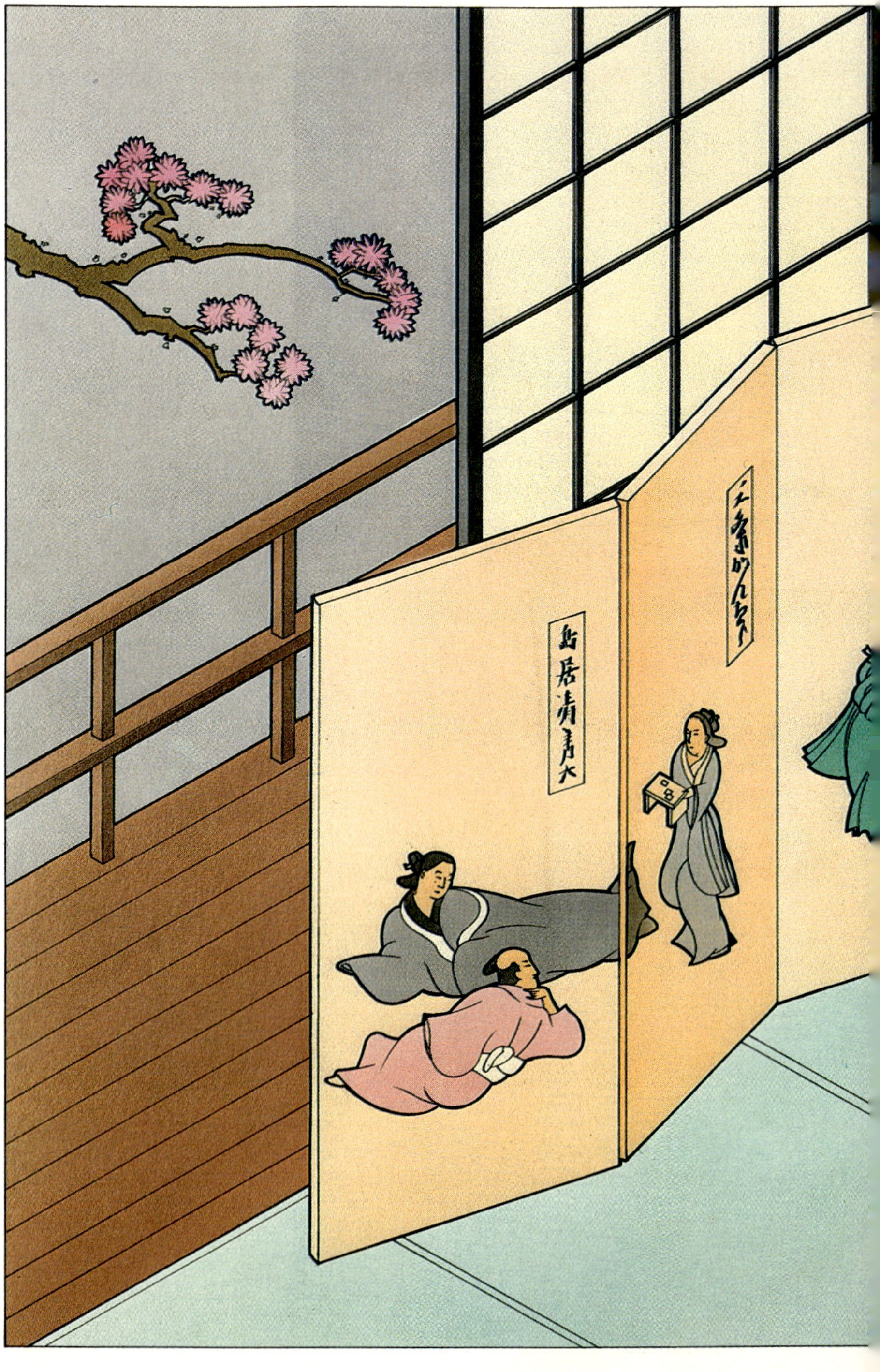

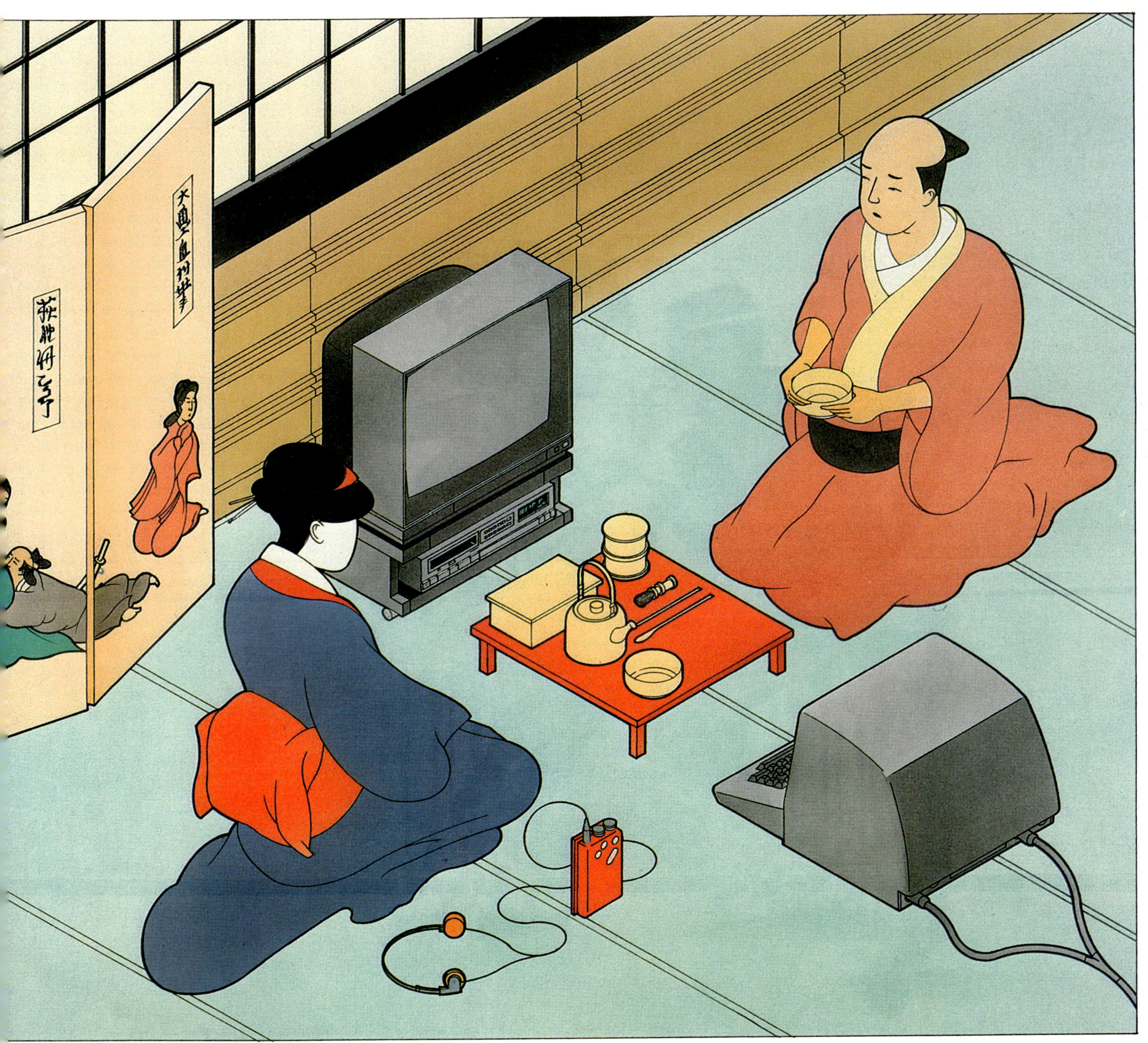

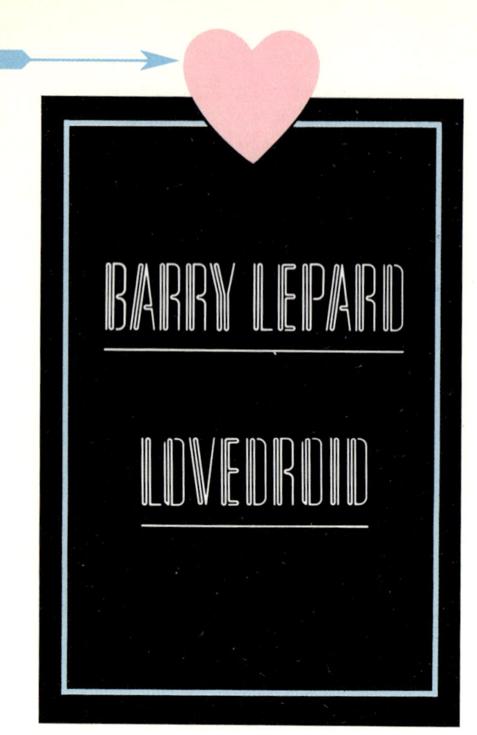
BARRY LEPARD
LOVEDROID

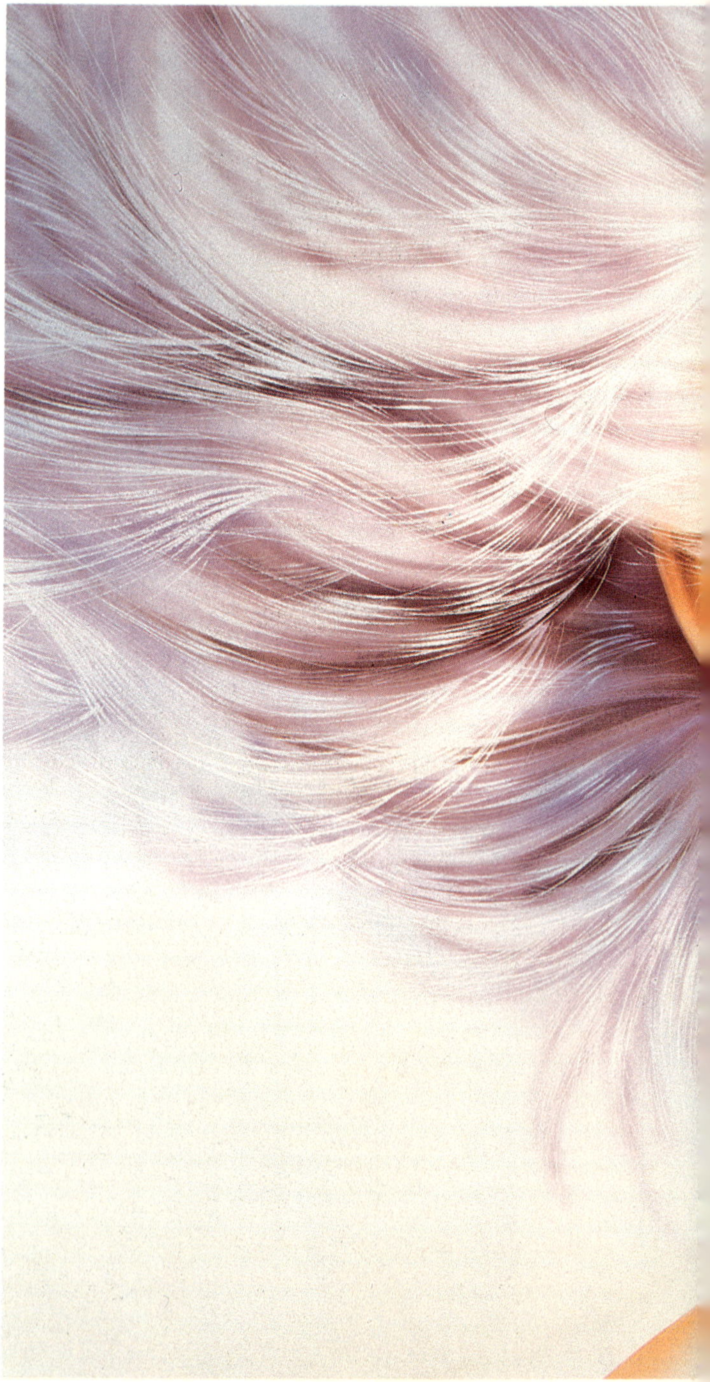

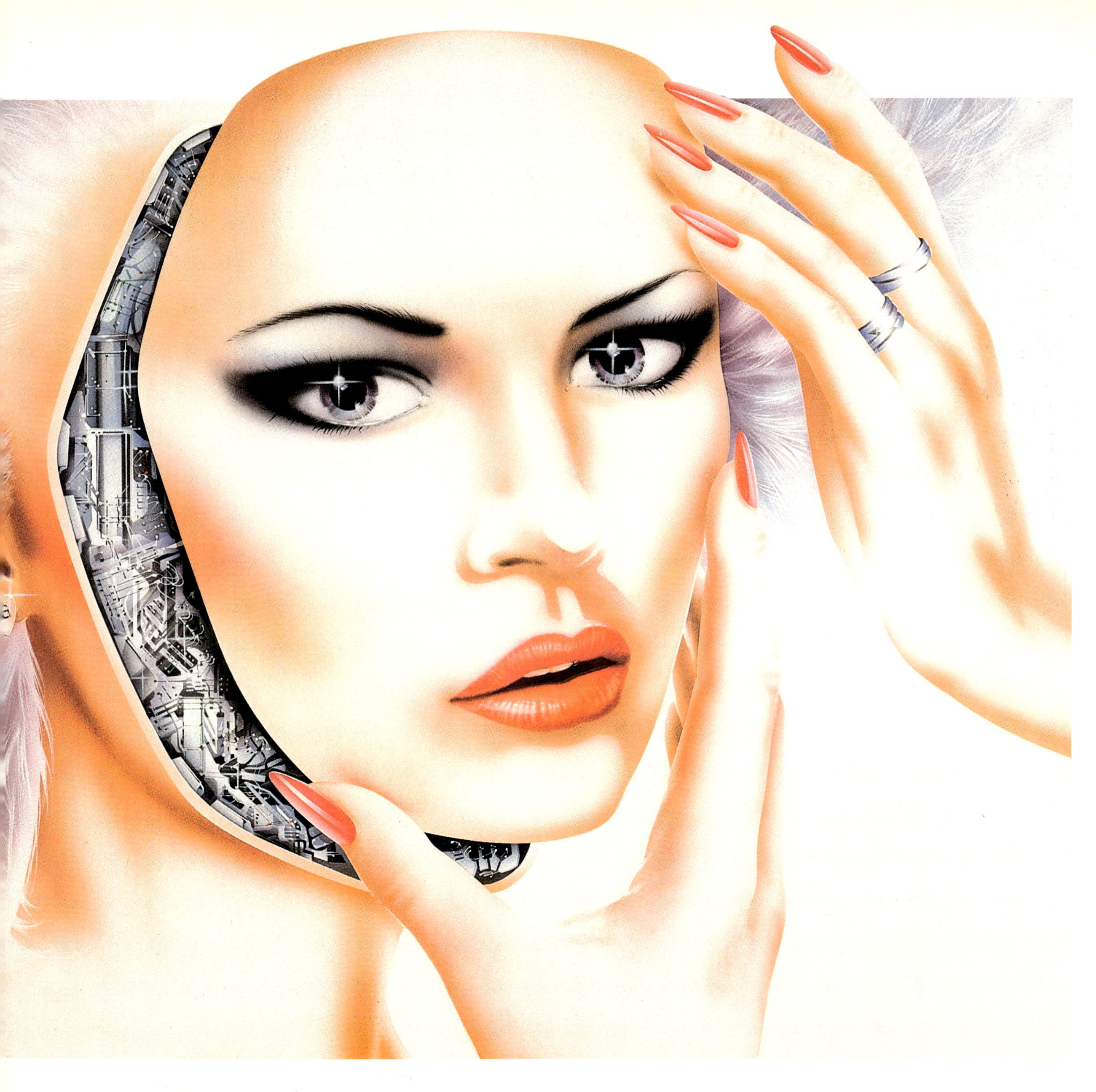

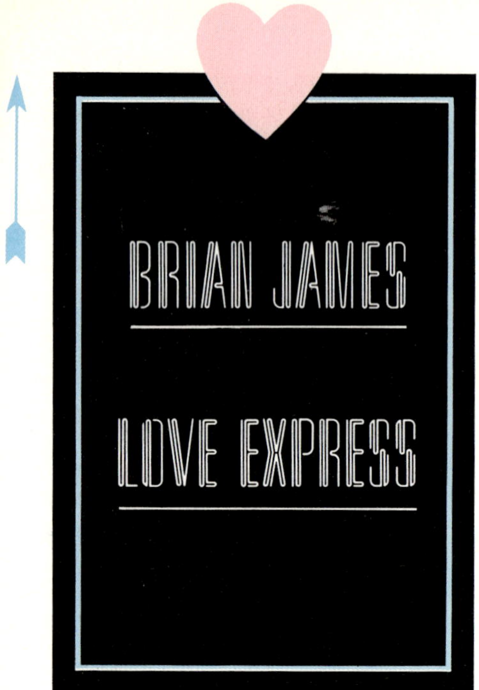
BRIAN JAMES
LOVE EXPRESS

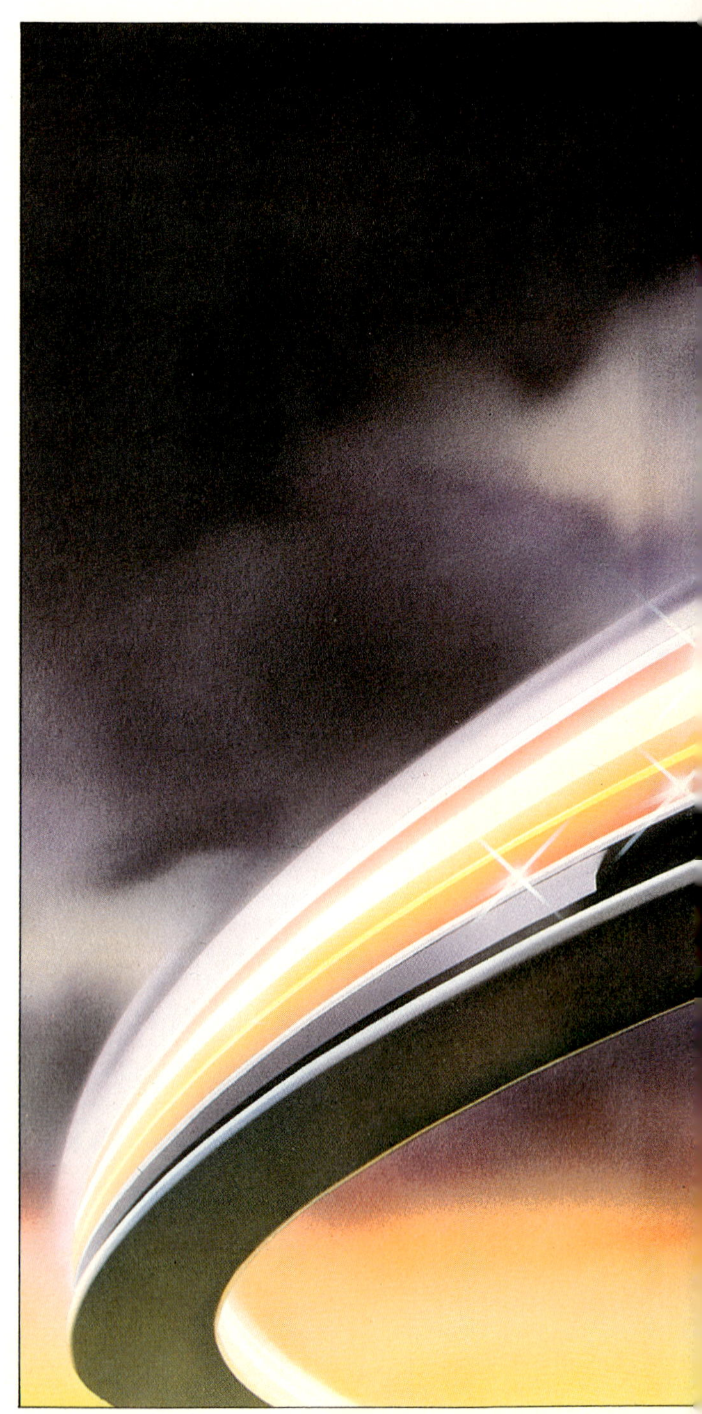

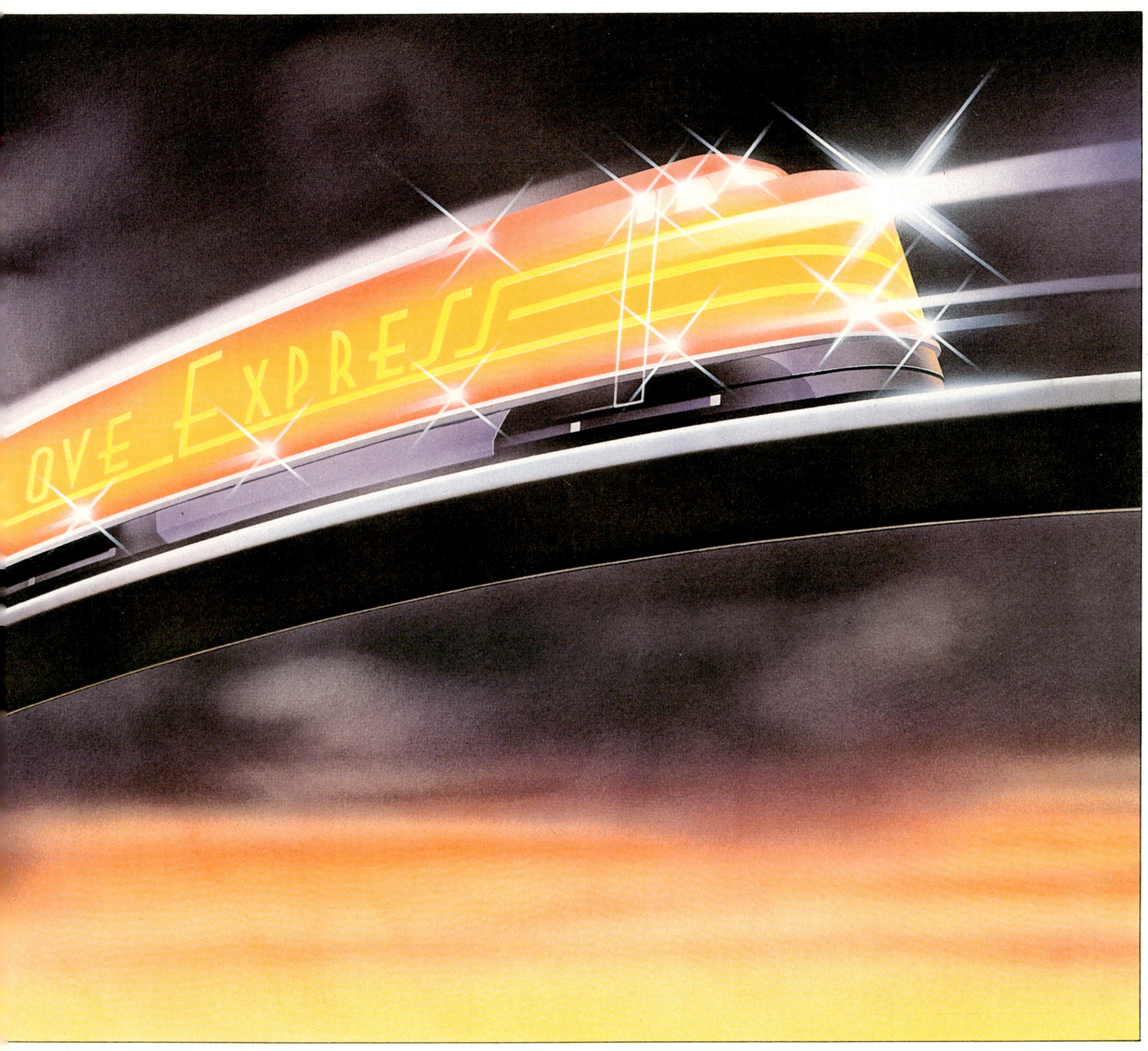
OVE EXPRESS

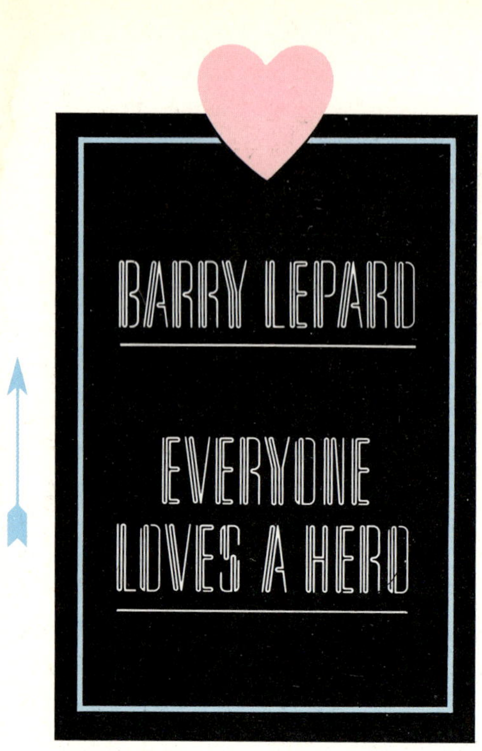
BARRY LEPARD
EVERYONE
LOVES A HERO

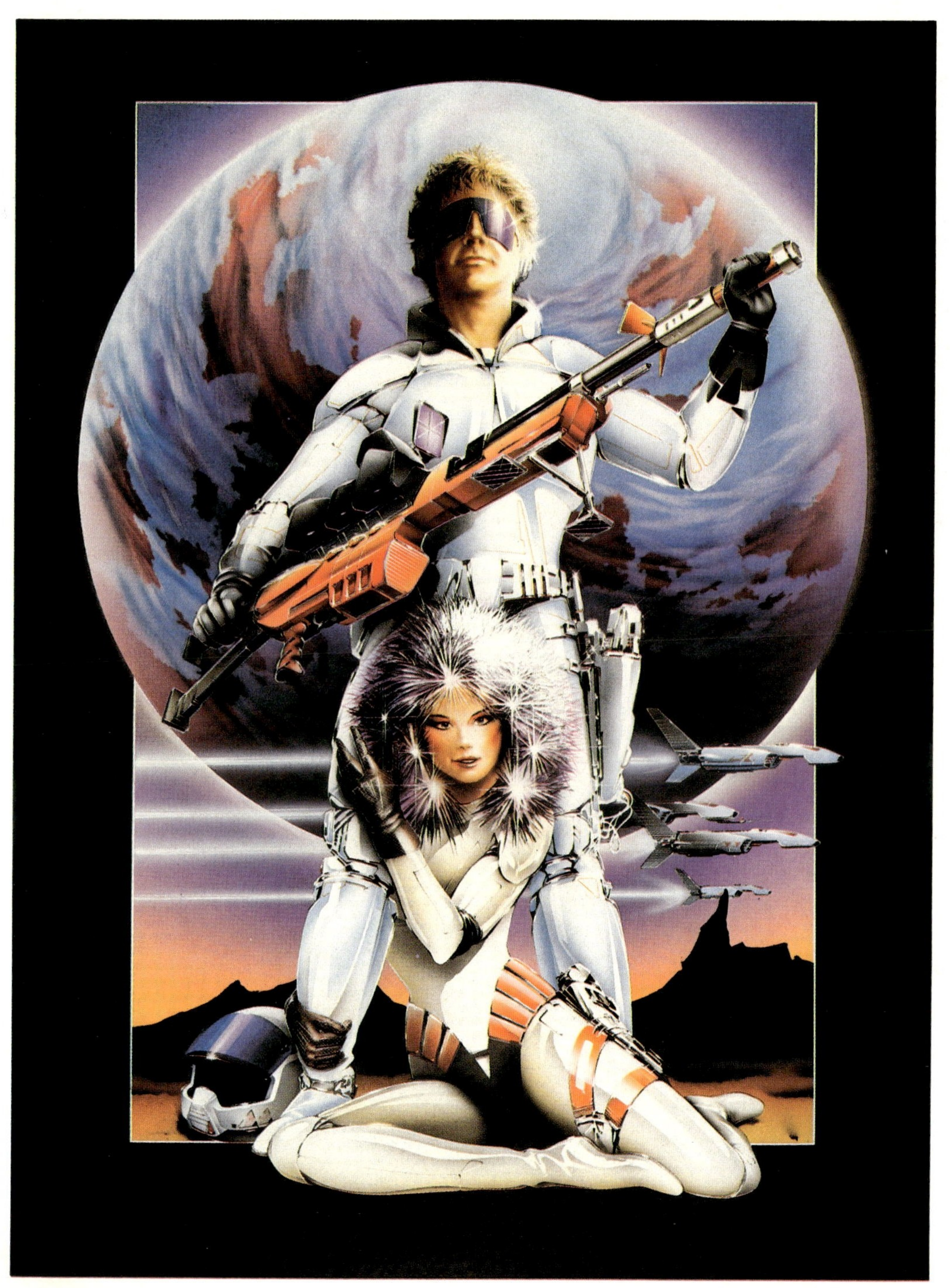

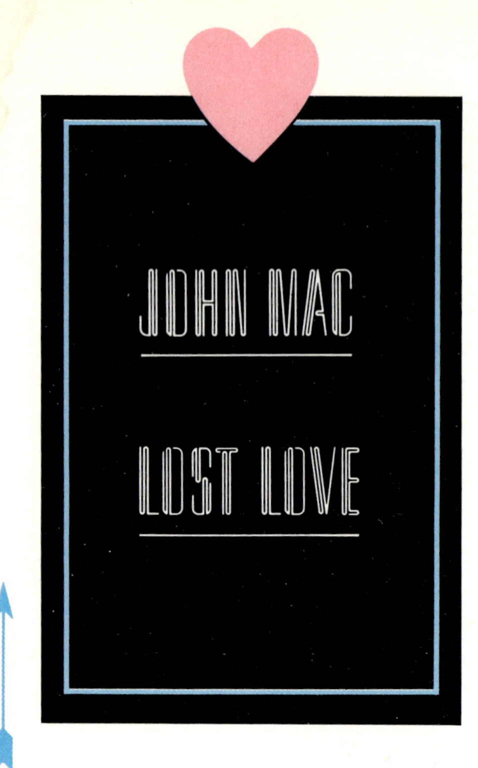

I'M NEVER GOING TO SEE HIM.... EVER AGAIN!

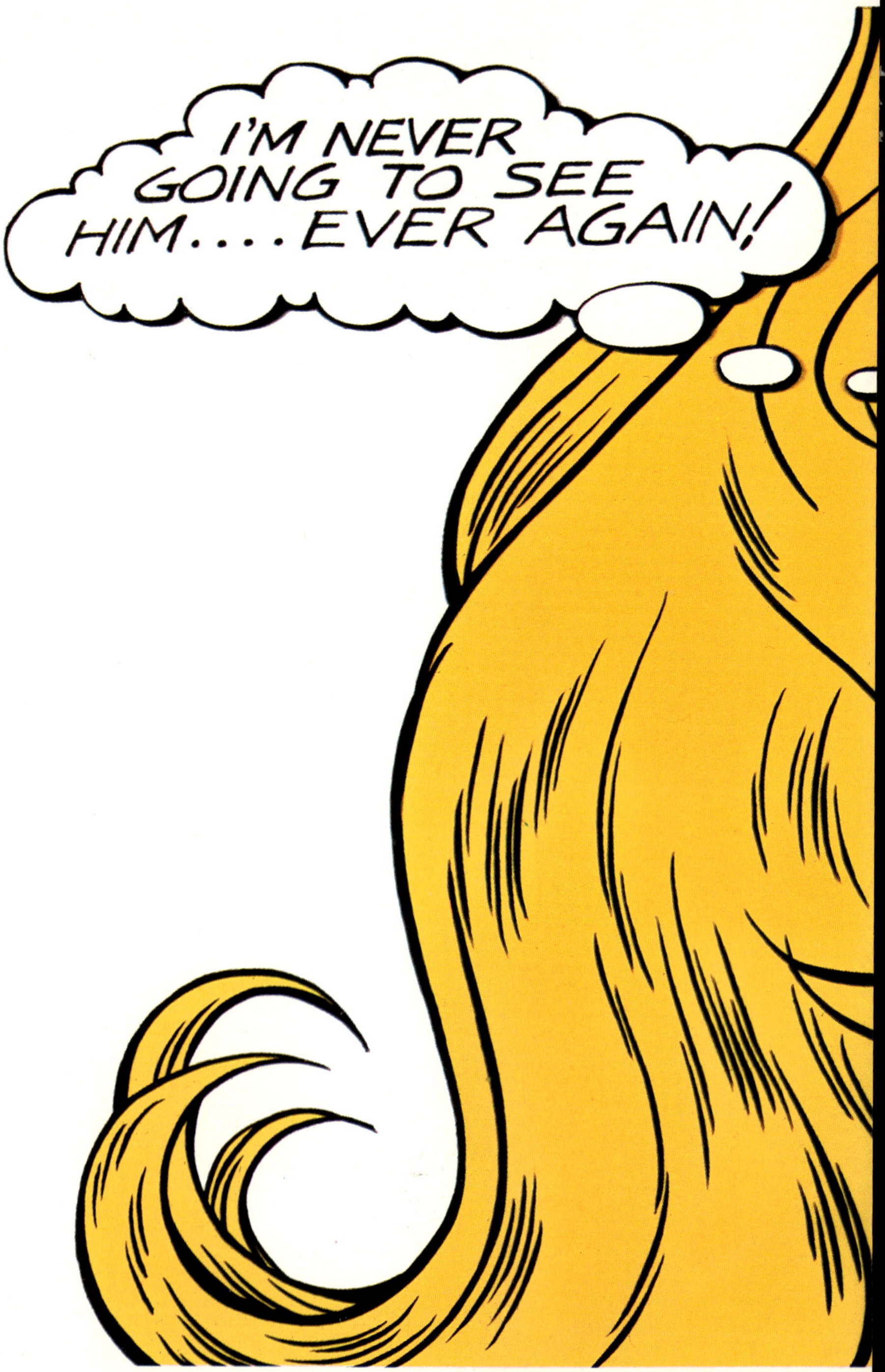

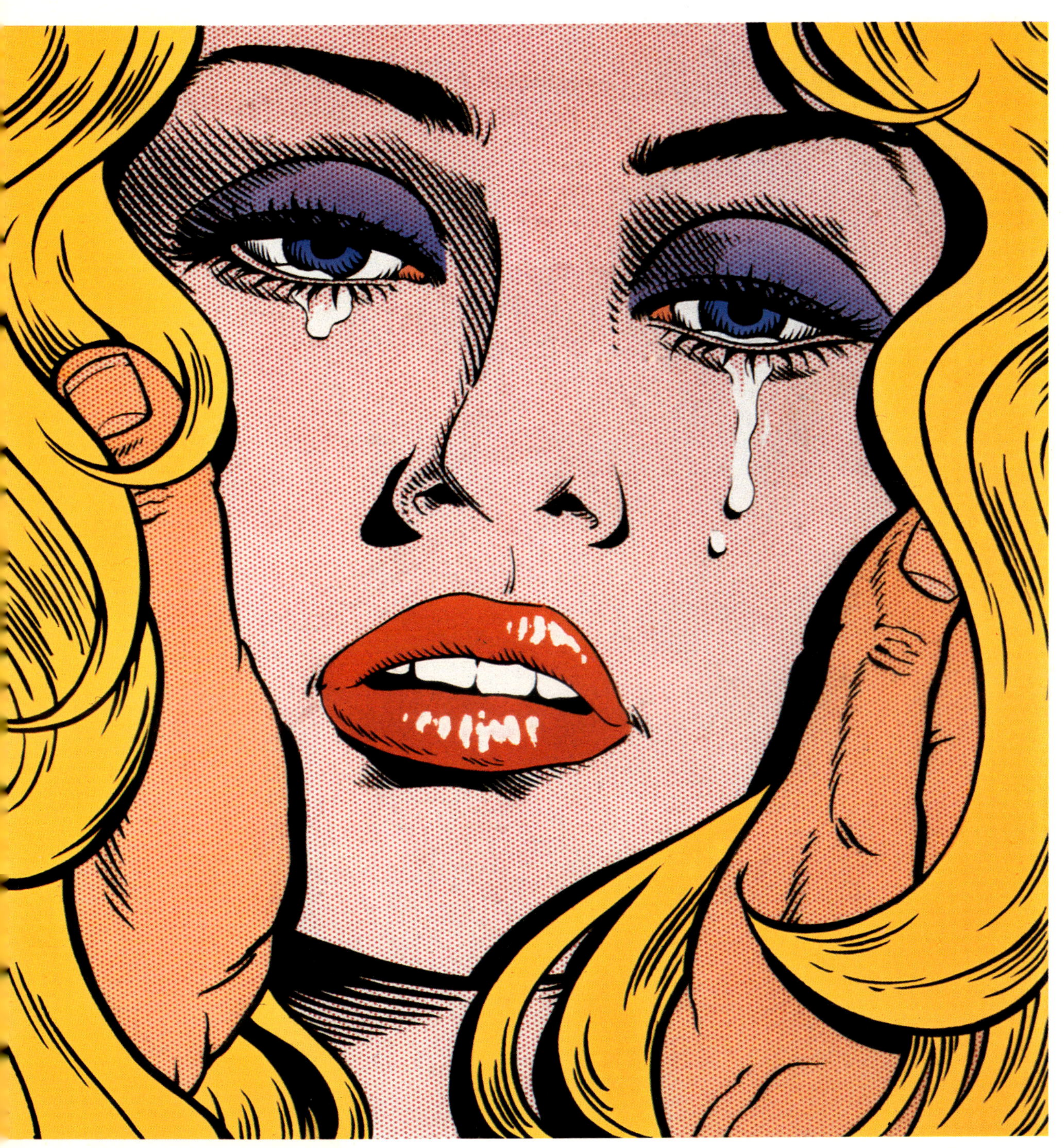

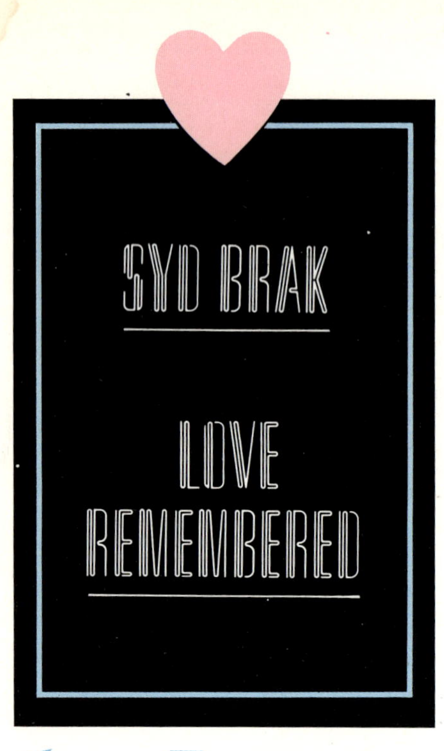
SYD BRAK
LOVE
REMEMBERED

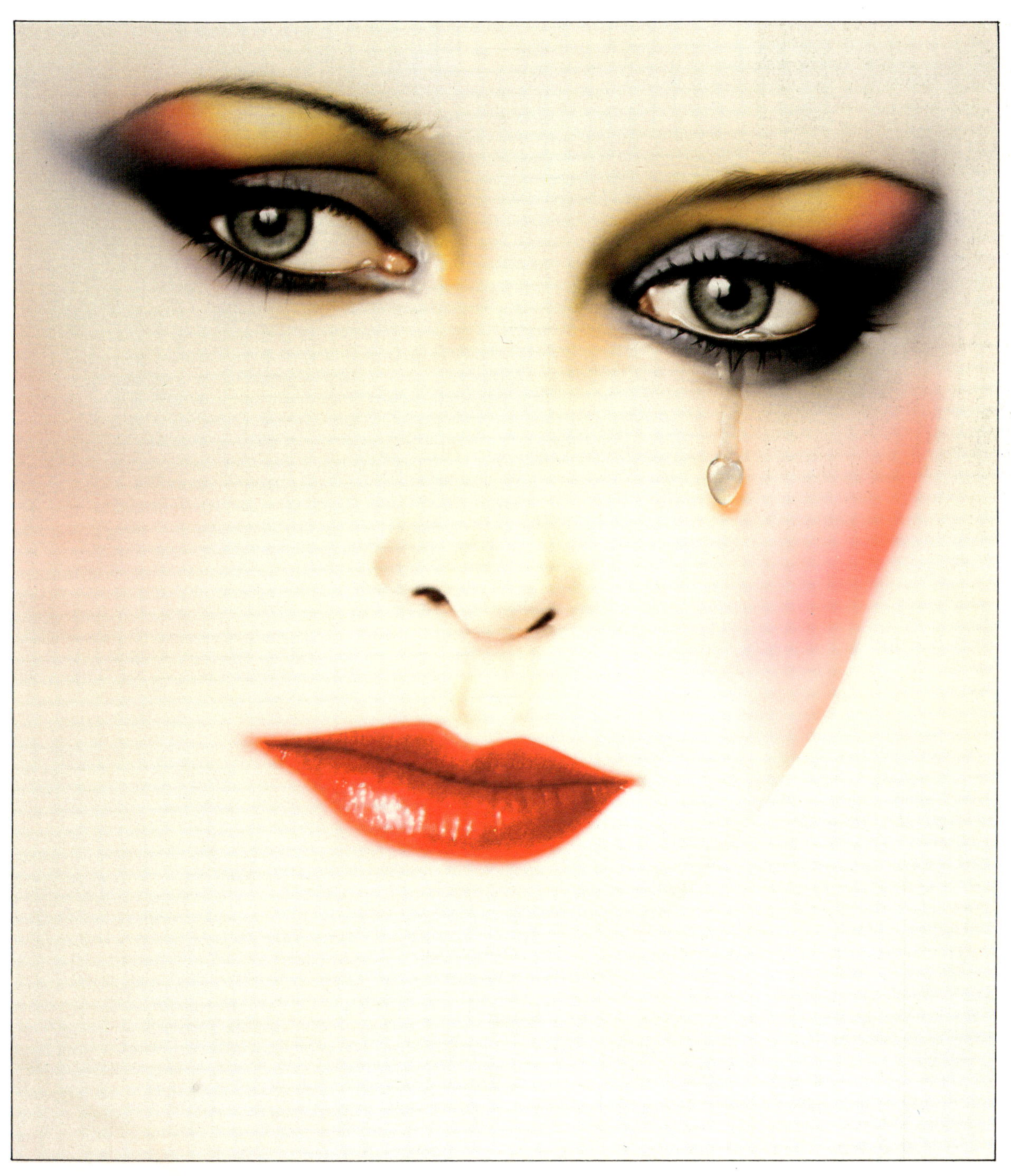

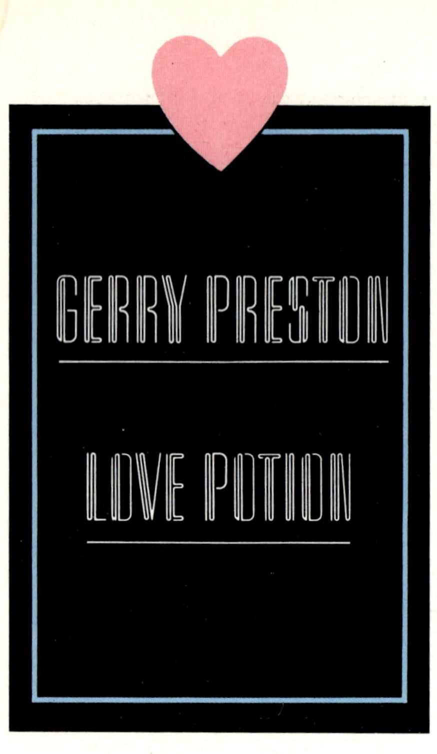
GERRY PRESTON
LOVE POTION

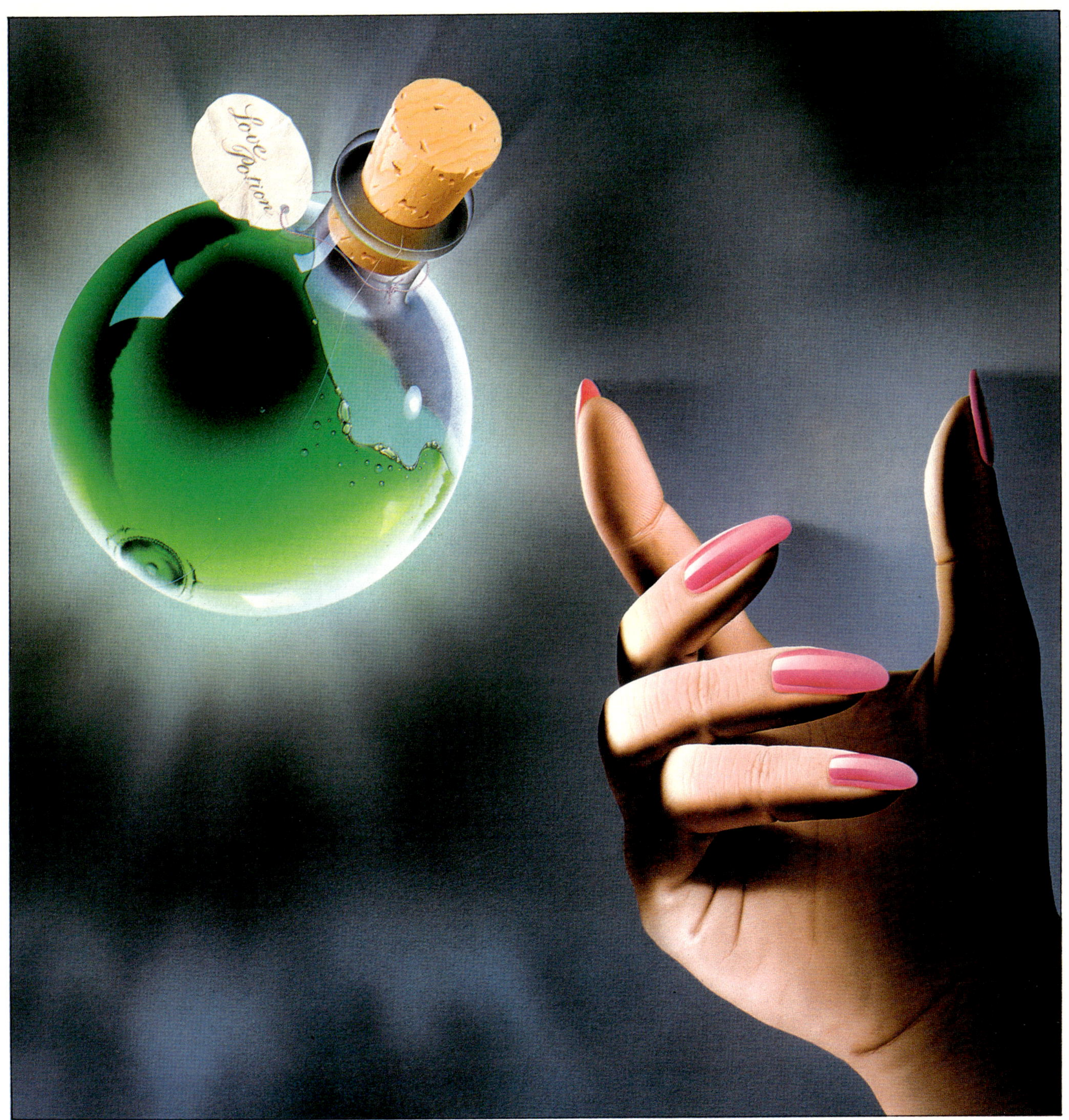
Love Potion